Brexit

# A Nation In Denial

A commentary of the trials and tribulations of;

Getting It Done

Author:     Peter E Gray

Publishing details

Date : May 2020

Isbn-  9798637226030

EAN-  xxxxxxxxxx

Copyright©  Peter E Gray (2020)

Author :     Peter E Gray

**Acknowledgments;**

To the valuable contributions made by those participating in interviews and discussions.

Thank you.

Also to those who participated without knowing it.

Sorry.

Elisa Kenton-Howells MA. BA(hons) Editor.

For Patience and understanding.


All revenues after costs to;

The homeless people of Peterborough.

# Contents

## Foreword

Having retired as a university lecturer in 2017, many research avenues dematerialised. As such so did the opportunity to produce academic papers relating to prediction of, and influential factors, determining shifts in voting habits. Initial thoughts were to seize the opportunity, to have my own platform on a subject very close to my heart, "Brexit". Where I could express personal opinions, without having to balance the content with a raft of other arguments, views and perspectives. The result of the referendum was a shock, having informed expectations of a small but significant remain result.

Essentially the burning question remains. How did I and many academic colleagues, David Cameron and George Osborne get it wrong. Perhaps our judgment was clouded by our own innate beliefs? As an academic it would be difficult to pursue a path that enhances only one of two perspectives. As such, chapter 2 "The current state play" seeks to determine which path should be pursued. Either remain or leave, no soft options, although perhaps some element of reasoned compromise should be considered, but nevertheless a re-evaluation of my own position.

Chapter 2. Commences with, two "time old" student favourite business analysis models. Known as SWOT (Strengths Weaknesses Opportunities Threats) and STEEPLE (Sociological Technological Economical Environmental Political Legalistic Ethical). The aim here being to provide a reasoned basis for taking either one side, or the other. Ultimately this analysis confirmed pre held beliefs sufficiently, to feel comfortable taking only one side of the argument, whilst being critical of the other.

Some of the earlier parts of this commentary deal with emerging developments, within the news media and political lobbies from local, national and international sources. In the development of this narrative, it had become clear that many of the dates of events were very significant. This in terms of; relevance to potential future readers, as well as demonstrating on occasion how quickly the political scene can change. As such the latter commentary becomes something, of a quasi diary, Whilst still maintaining a more conventional structure. where significant events are still marked by chapters as opposed to just specific dates.

As this narrative/commentary approached 24,000 words and a general election had been called again, it had become evident that "this story" would not be ending sometime soon! Not wishing to compete with Tolstoy's War and peace, in terms of word count. This precipitating a decision to conclude this commentary at a point when the dust had settled on the 2019 general election. Thus providing some clear direction that could be applied to the next stage of the journey.

The concluding chapter 5. "Revelations" makes a range predicted outcomes for the forthcoming 2020's. This could potentially lay the foundations of a sequel! To this publication, God help us!

**Draft copy comments from friends and colleagues**;

Jane

"I found it to be quite sarcastic in nature, but still an interesting read. I particularly liked the later half of the commentary "the diary part" this shows how dynamic and changeable the whole situation was".

David

"Thanks for letting me read this before publication. Good luck with it and will be even more worth reading in 5 years time".

Pam

"The attacks on Trump and Boris Johnson in particular using the remark "clown" totally ignores the fact that Boris is a highly educated academic with a number of acclaimed literary works and the speaker of at least four languages. Totally out of order in my view"

John

"Your reference to the bailout of Thomas Cook business is typical of one rule for them and another for the rest of us. When Barnier talks about a level playing field on state subsidy during negotiations, he should be putting his own house in order".

Elisa

I have just finished reading this and I think it is brilliant. I read it with an interest for learning, a smile at many of your offhand comments, laughed out loud at the poignancy and humour of your commentary, and had a tear in my eye when I read of the genuine regret and sense of bereavement that you feel over the whole Brexit event in history and its potential impact on the future. Thank you for sharing this with me.

# Chapter 1

## Introduction and background

The EU referendum was enshrined in the Conservative party manifesto of 2015, when David Cameron was Prime minister and leader of the Conservative party. True to his word David Cameron delivered the referendum in June 2016. The resultant voting paper was clearly defined as; leave the EU, or remain in the EU. There were no predetermined majority criteria, just a straight win from either side would suffice to make the decision leave or remain. No ambiguities or confusion, "simples" as Sergei the meerkat would say.

The result if anyone needs reminding was 37% of the electorate voted to leave whilst 35% voted to remain, with 28% of the electorate either unable to decide or not wishing to participate. These very figures have, and still do, lead to many a debate. Where those who consider themselves winners, will regard the figures as definitive, democratic and sacrosanct. Whilst the so called losers could realistically question their validity citing the result as marginal, unsafe, undemocratic and not representative of a true majority. A true majority is defined as more than 50% of a given population, in this case the total electorate. As such 37% falls far short of that criterion. However it can be argued that statistically 37% vs. 35% of a given population has a greater than 90% probability of reflecting an accurate outcome had all the electorate voted. If that risk factor were to be applied to flying in an aircraft then most of the airports in the world would close down due to the absence of customers.

The primary catalyst leading to this narrative was the result of the 2016 European Union referendum. At the time my personal involvement with international affairs was as an associate lecturer in international relations and economics with the Northampton University Business School. Over many years prior to the referendum vote, I had conducted a multitude of seminars, lectures and research activities based on; leave or remain issues. These were programme elements with several universities, for students on graduate and postgraduate courses.

As such experiential involvement had drawn a reasoned personal conclusion that, although any referendum would likely be close, there existed a small, but significant skew towards remain. The outcome was, as is now evident, exactly the reverse.

Initial thinking on this result was that of, "remainer" complacency i.e. didn't bother to vote because they considered that remaining would be the outcome. This line of thought could reasonably also apply to Brexiteers.

Some early research in this area revealed that remainer complacency was far from the case, the relatively small sample of non voters surveyed, revealed results closely mirroring those of the referendum. Closer examination of these results also revealed that applying extremes of age demonstrated very significantly different outcomes. Over 60s it would seem favoured Brexit to circa 70%. Whereas 16 to 24 year olds outcomes were the almost exact reverse i.e. 70% remain. People who didn't vote were typically harder to find in the over 60s group, than in any other group even though the 16 to 24 group of which those 16 to 18 years were not eligible to vote. In general terms demonstrating that the older generations are considerably more likely to vote than the younger electorate. Although these samples were far from adequate to provide more definitive answers, for academic purposes. But does beg the question did the 60 plus generation decide the outcome of the referendum?

Many interviews and discussions were carried out to help inform this narrative, interviews that were both overt and covert in nature. Mostly covert as a result of considerable hostility encountered from direct or challenging questioning. Discussions took much the same line, akin to throwing a brick into a pond and watching the effects of the ripples. The conclusion of this introduction is based around a question posed by an interviewee who was a well informed, engaging and non hostile Brexit supporter. The interviewee posed the question as follows:

> "I don't want any pie in the sky statistics, economic case studies, financial implications or political bias. Why do you personally want to remain in the European union"?.

The following response was provided:

> "I have been on this planet for 71 years now, 45 of those years have been as an EU citizen. One of the post war baby boomers, a secondary modern educated boy from a small town, council estate. That progressed to an apprenticeship in a large engineering company, underpinned by block release to a local technical college. Culminating in both

*practical skills and academic skills in manufacturing engineering.*

*Six years on, the EEC (European Economic Community). 1974 referendum, took the UK into the European Community. Since that time I have never been unemployed, and along with my wife we own our house, have two children both of whom have graduate and postgraduate qualifications and professional employment commensurate with their qualifications. We have been round the world twice, once by ship and once by plane. Having visited 56 different countries including most of those in Europe. My grandfather fought in the First World War, my father fought in the second world war. The legacy of peace afforded by them and their peers has meant that the trauma of war has not darkened mine, or my family's doorstep. We have had no big benefactors; everything has been achieved by work and opportunity. Europe is a growing and diverse continent. Why would I want to leave the EU? I am a European."*

This lady's question, for me was quite profound, having a technical and business management background. This question did not allow my usual approach i.e. measure, analyse, evaluate, prove etc. On the face of it my answer may seem a little pompous and self fulfilling, I was merely offering my experience as fairly typical of my peers and my generation. As such this answer provided an alternative perspective, whilst still being built on a reasoned argument.

# Chapter 2

## 2016 The current state of play

The following analysis examines the state of play around the time of the referendum. This built around two well used business analysis techniques, STEEPLE and SWOT. To be more specific STEEPLE;

> **S**ociological
> **T**echnological
> **E**conomic,
> **E**nvironmental,
> **P**olitical,
> **L**egalistic
> **E**thical

This provides a framework of the key factors affecting the most common elements of human life. Whilst SWOT considers;

> **S**trengths
> **W**eaknesses
> **O**pportunities
> **T**hreats

Combined, these two "tools" are representative of the so called journey concept, which provides the third dimension of time;

Where are we now
Where do we want to be
How are we going to get there
When do we need to be there
What are the risks
How can these risks mitigated

STEEPLE considers the where are we now, and closely linked to both the strengths and opportunities associated with SWOT. It looks at the potential destinations (Opportunities) afforded by identified (Strengths) and (Weaknesses) from the STEEPLE analysis, whilst taking account of the risks (Threats) associated with a selected destination, or combinations of destinations. Clearly there are many further nuances to these analysis tools, but in general terms these key elements are adequate for the purposes of this publication, which is not intended as academic engagement.

## STEEPLE analysis

### Sociological

English has become the second language of the EU, certainly within the business community. Likely this has more to do with the Americans than the British, but clearly an advantage with more than 20 different languages being spoken within the EU. This not only giving an ability to communicate with a high proportion of Europeans, but also provides a catalyst for others to communicate with each other, for example French to Polish or German to Spanish. A key factor leading to further promotion of the English language on a global scale.

Those with European passports can Live, work, holiday in EU countries without time or financial constraints. This by many is considered to be a disadvantage to EU membership, in that EU nationals are taking jobs that could otherwise be taken by UK nationals. Surely though, any withdrawal of this apparent privilege would likely result in reciprocal withdrawal by the EU. Thereby many thousands of expatriates could be forced to return to the UK.

More rigorous boarder control will not stop the so "called boat people," "truck hoppers," "tunnel walkers" etc. Whether they are economic migrants or asylum seekers, but for the forbearance of the French, Camp Calais, could so easily become Camp Dover.

Student exchanges, such as ERASMUS (European Regions Action Scheme for the Mobility of University Students) could potentially end with Brexit, being an EU sponsored scheme, to the tune of €30 billion plus each year. Whilst other reciprocal educational arrangements currently that operate on a good will basis, being mutually beneficial whichever way exchanges take place. It is highly unlikely all of these educational opportunities would be lost, particularly those involving research activities. Academics would likely continue on a verbal basis, barring official secrets of course, they tend to have little respect for borders, boundaries and politics. More likely it would just become more formalised in terms of financial arrangements, Visas, contracts etc. Whilst potentially reducing up take to some extent, by way of frustration with red tape and general bureaucracy.

The EU consistently sponsors one off educational development actives in collaboration with professional bodies such as the CMI Chartered Management Institute, Further education colleges etc. Education is the cornerstone to the EU's thinking on social, academic and economic development.

Healthcare provision in the form of E111 (EHIC) European Health Insurance Card, and other reciprocal medical arrangements. Quite frequently medical procurement by the NHS takes place with several EU countries, where patients are treated, to cover lack of capacity within the NHS or specialist procedures, such as proton beam treatment for cancer.

The UK still operates border controls which can theoretically prevent any entry to the country by any people other than those with a valid EU passport. Unlike most countries in the EU both the UK and Eire did not sign up to the Schengen agreement. Those that did sign up do not have borders other than those external to the EU. With Eire and the UK not signed up to Schengen this could help in a no deal situation. I that anyone travelling from say France to Eire would be subject to border control.

Security cooperation may likely be compromised, not only from the exchange of information perspective, but the potential loss of the European arrest warrant and the jurisdiction of the European court of Justice. Or indeed extradition arrangements.

Opportunities from Brexit to rebuild the fishing industry and communities that have been decimated by unfair allocations of fishing rights from the EU. The social benefits are very clear, although economically insignificant. Many would suggest this argument should have been resolved years ago, with a whole sequence of governments of different persuasions failing to grasp the nettle.

Work visas are likely to become mandatory regardless of deal or no deal. These may or may not be reciprocal agreements as part of the "final deal". The UK tends currently to favour the Australian points system.

## Technological

Leaving the EU means leaving joint projects like Galileo the European global positioning system. Galileo is a key project of the ESA European Space Agency, designed as an alternative to the American GPS. The concept of Galileo is to be a civil system as opposed to the American military system, which potentially could be switched off at any time, if the USA military decided so. The UK has already contributed €1.4 billion to the total €10.5 billion cost to date not including launch vehicle costs. During Brexit negotiations in August 2018 the British government suggested that the UK would be developing its own system. Galileo has been 12 years in the making and the UK doesn't have its own launch vehicle. Precipitating a need to rely on ESA, the Americans, India or maybe China for the heavy lifting. The likelihood of the UK building its own GPS in the next five years is very slim, despite the availability of world leading technology.

The UK is however, at the forefront of satellite design and manufacture, so the capability certainly exists. Other emerging technologies such as autonomous motorised transport are dependent on very accurate and reliable GPS navigation.

CERN (in French *Conseil Européen pour la Recherche Nucléaire)* another large predominately European project of which the UK is an active participant. This is the world's largest Hadron collider. Apart from proving the existence of the Higgs-Boson particle, potential tangible benefits are cheap, clean and safe energy. Although predominantly a European project it is highly unlikely that UK involvement will change significantly, currently making the second largest contribution €150m, behind Germany at around €210m for 2019, which is based on GDP (Gross Domestic Product).

These types of projects can be so expensive that potentially only China and the USA could financially support them. In present day terms it cost the USA around $300 billion dollars to put Neil Armstrong on the moon. Going it alone very often is not an option, with future projects potentially requiring even wider international commitment.

Vertical horticulture/farming, may well be the way we feed the world in the future. Very large buildings with a hundred or more levels in totally controlled environments, no season's, no soil, no weed killers, automated harvesting and little involvement of human beings. From an environmental perspective these "food factories" consume carbon dioxide like it is "going out of fashion." Currently it would seem the Dutch are world leaders in this technology, with the UK certainly engaging with this innovative approach to food production.

Artificial Intelligence (AI) has amazing potential, not only for low skilled jobs such as picking fruit by controlling robotic machines, but also very highly skilled work. Recent research (December 2019) demonstrated that AI evaluation of CT scans for breast cancer were not only much quicker, but just as accurate and some cases more accurate than 2 highly skilled clinicians. Again the UK is at the cutting edge with this technology,

Galileo, ESA, AI and countless other joint ventures with the Universities, advanced medical treatments such as proton beam cancer treatment. It is likely, if the UK wishes to continue with these projects then there will be a price to pay not only financially, but in terms of collaboration and education, both key areas for investment and encouragement.

**Economic**

Collectively the EU is the second largest trading power in the world at 17.9 T$usd with the USA at 18.6 T$ usd and China 12.2 T$usd (Trillion United States Dollars)

Through membership of the EU, the UK has trading arrangements with the ECOWAS (Economic Community Of West African States) 15 countries in all. Along with, Canada, Japan, Brazil, Norway etc. As well as access to other world trade opportunities through the WTO (World Trade Organisation)

The UK trades at 2.7 T$usd quite small in comparison. Perhaps those of a more optimistic disposition believe the rest of the world will be knocking on the UK'S door begging to do business, once it is freed of the shackles of those nasty Europeans.

In general terms 17.9 t$usd (EU) gives considerably more leverage than 2.7 T$usd (UK)

Unfortunately for the "European project", Brexit means a reduction their GDP (Gross Domestic Product) to circa 15.2 T$usd. Potentially opening the door for the Chinese to slip into second place in the world trade pecking order.

Currently the UK is in fifth place as an individual country behind; USA, China, Japan and Germany. Should Scotland separate from the UK then it is likely that the remaining UK would be relegated to 7th place behind France and India. Although this could happen without the loss of Scotland if the promised utopia doesn't materialise.

Generous subsidies to agriculture, in the form of the CAP (Common Agricultural Policy) has made food relatively inexpensive. The absence of Government commitment as to how these subsidies will be replaced, has put a question mark on future costs of living.

Many UK based companies are currently scaling back their investments in the UK i.e. Honda, Nissan, Toyota, Sony and many smaller organisations, moving some their activities to mainland Europe and the far east. So why did these companies set up in the UK in first place? The UK was seen as the gateway to Europe, with excellent sea, road, rail links to northern, southern and eastern Europe.

UK trade with the EU represents about 50% of GDP i.e. 1.35 T$us. The converse of this the EU exports to the UK circa 1.4 T$us slightly more. In the unlikely event that all trade with the EU were to cease, then the UK would loose circa 50% of its trade i.e. 1.35T$us. In a reciprocated scenario the EU would loose 1.4T$us, when considered against 17.9Tusd or in percentage terms 7.9% which when shared between 27 countries, becomes of little significance.

A trade deal with the USA will likely include aspects of the NHS, with an annual spend of over £300 billion, that is not something the Americans will want to miss out on.

**Environmental**

The Paris accord on $CO_2$ reduction, potentially a step in the right direction. Unfortunately President Trump has withdrawn from this agreement, dismissing global warming as scare mongering and false news. Unfortunately this means the world's largest polluter the USA is not committed to carbon reduction. In fact may even add further to the problem, by reopening coal mining facilities.

Many infrastructure projects are financed by the EU via financial incentives towards town bypasses, public transport improvements and energy reduction projects.

Michael Gove Environment Minister has devised strategies to help farmers with sustainability practices and subsidies to support the protection of wildlife. How this will be paid for is not quite so clear at the time of writing. Or indeed how this fits with proposed UK food security.

UK Government support for the installation of domestic and commercial solar panel systems. As well wind turbines many thousands of them offshore such as the Thames estuary, the Wash etc. Many of these currently very successful, offsetting a reducing reliance on fossil fuels.

Many UK commitments to the environment go beyond those of the EU. But what of the consequences if the UK nails its flag to the American pole?

**Political**

EU support against the Russian poisoning activities and participation in retaliatory actions, such as sanctions on trade and withdrawal of co-operation with the Russians.

The EU is well placed to stand up to Russian aggression, both militarily and economically. Yes the UK has a nuclear deterrent, but a sledge hammer it not much good for cracking nuts. Particularly when they also have Nuclear weapons.

Co-operation with international terrorism and intelligence sharing, could potentially be undermined by Brexit.

French support with the loan of aircraft carriers to the Royal Navy relating to delays of building and commissioning the UK'S latest aircraft carriers. Although Joint NATO membership and European military exercises and development of the Euro fighter could potentially keep the wheels lubricated, subject to Mr Trumps whims.

**Legalistic**

EJC (European Court of Justice) and the ECHR (European Court of Human Rights) arguably the benchmark for global human rights legislation. has been evident as a backstop to preventing many injustices. For example the extradition of an asperger's inflicted computer hacker Gary McKinnon, or a young boy Ashya king with terminal cancer. who's parents wanted to try proton beam treatment in the Czech Republic, but refused by

British bureaucracy, to date the little lad survives (2018) with no signs of cancer.

The following were all instigated resultant from EU membership;

The National minimum wage, which the conservative opposition of the time suggested it would bankrupt hundreds of companies.

The introduction of; Working time directive, payment for bank holidays, considerable health and safety legislation.

Product quality verification EC mark for standards on manufactured or imported goods.

The non acceptance of American chlorine washed chicken or hormone fed beef.

Post Brexit, how much of EU legislation will be revoked, revised or replaced?


**Ethical**

In terms of Culture and ethics most European nations share closely aligned values and a sense of fair play. It could be said in general terms the EU leads the world in ethical business practices, respect for intellectual property, engaging and involvement in corporate governance and the recognition of all stakeholders in the broadest sense of the term. Workers counsels, partnership schemes, profit sharing and added value reward schemes. Maternity and paternity leave. As well as supporting and underpinning ground-breaking legislation on human rights.

Purchases and sales to only businesses sharing the same ethical values and fair trade principles. Avoiding engagement with companies that sell arms or tobacco products.

Whilst many of these concepts are policy as opposed to legislation, much has been done in many areas to apply the principles. This supported by emergent legislation and indeed underpinned by the Adam Smith Institute, a world leading think tank.

UK alignment with a "Trump USA" could seriously undermine much of the thinking and principles underpinning these concepts.

# **SWOT** (UK)

## **Strengths**

English is the most widely spoken language, and certainly in the business sector.

A relatively strong economy, $5^{th}$ globally.

Two universities in the top 5 universities in the world

Highly acclaimed qualifications and teaching

An innovative culture.

Reputation as international peacemakers/keepers

Leading members of the United Nations

## **Weaknesses**

Reluctance to learn foreign languages

Crumbling infrastructure

Health care with diminishing and falling standards

High reliance on foreign workers

Limited opportunities outside current trading circles

Not so good at putting innovative ideas into practice

The ERG (European Research Group) hell bent on sabotaging the European project. Which does not make for good relations or trade deals with the EU

Relatively Small GDP as an independent i.e. relatively small leverage.

## Opportunities

"A fantastic trade deal with the USA" (Boris Johnson) and of course a fantastic deal with the EU. All in 11 months.

To reengage with 40 smaller countries on free trade deals lost to Brexit.

To "make our own rules" but is the reality?

## Threats

Game changing trade deals take an average of five to seven years.

A no deal Brexit.

USA not accepting the UKs red lines ie NHS, chlorinated chicken, etc.

No apparent post Brexit planning with defined objectives, underpinned with expected and potential outcomes

The demise of the UK; ie Scottish independence, reunification of Ireland.

The loss of free trade deals with 40 other countries, complimentary to EU membership 67countries in all.

## Conclusion

Whilst this analysis is quite limited it does pickup on the key factors pertaining to the position at the time of writing and the purpose for which it was intended. There are many "what ifs" and nuances that could be developed considerably, but at the risk of becoming so conjugated that the true purpose becomes obscured.

Key factors;

The losses in free trade agreements with around 67 countries could be catastrophic.

The chances of recovering those or better agreements in the short or medium term are next to non existent.

Much emphasis has been placed on a deal with the USA

At this point there are no apparent outline plans for this, either in context or content.

Many "too large for one country" projects are at risk.

The UK may need to stay onboard with these, but there will clearly be a cost.

The benefits, not just potential savings of Brexit are yet to be quantified.

The risk to the stability and continuity of the United Kingdom as it stands today are immense.

The risk of failure of the "Brexit project" are both potentially catastrophic and plausible.

The foregoing analysis provides an overview "where we are now" i.e. pre Brexit. The following narrative considers potential benefits of a no deal Brexit, the most likely outcome at the time of writing.

Tax revenue (duty) on imports ie wine, spirits, tobacco, fragrances. Currently lost to the so called free market. Back to old days of duty free allowances ie 2 bottles of spirit, 4 bottles of wine and 200 cigarettes. This will likely create employment opportunities, in that people will be needed to collect these duties and of course to police the borders.

Tariffs on imports at an average of 10% based on WTO rules. The EU exports to the UK 1.4 Trillion $usd of goods each year.

Note: (international trade is measured in $usd)

Based on the average WTO tariff this would generate 140 billion $usd revenue for the UK treasury. More employment opportunities here, administering some 275 billion $usd of tariffs in different currencies. Perhaps this will provide jobs for redundant bank staff.

There are of course tariffs on UK exports of which currently there are 1.35 Trillion $usd to the EU. This would cost the UK based again on WTO average 10%, 135 billion $usd. Assuming the balance remains the same this leaves the UK with a surplus of 5 billion $usd, but of course that doesn't take account of the employment costs incurred.

Further tariffs with Japan, Canada, Norway, Liechtenstein, Iceland, Switzerland, the 18 West African agreement countries and about 16 other countries including Chile, Egypt, Denmark etc. All of these have free trade deals which are currently complementary to EU membership. Without extensive research, into the trade figures of 40 countries in total it is assumed imports and exports are pro rata with those of the EU and as such attract appropriate tariffs.

£9 billion net contributions to EU per annum will be saved, although it will take approximately 4 to 5 years to reap the benefits ie recovery of the exit deal of £39 billion. Plus other costs incurred as a result of leaving the EU.

Allocation of fishing rights will be much more in the UKs favour, this would likely provide a boost to the fishing industry. Slightly tempered with the loss of access to those fishing grounds deemed as European.

Substitute EU rules and regulations with those of the USA. President Trump likes his terms and conditions, "no deal is complete without them".

Less foreign workers in our hospitals, with all the new money available for the NHS and the 40 new hospitals that are coming on stream.

By the final exit date 31st December 2020 four years plus from the referendum. All the government's Brexit plans will start to materialise.

Many of the new nurses will be completing their training ready to take up their positions in the new hospitals

The new British Doctors will be more than half way through their training.

Farms and factories will all be totally mechanised and as such will not need foreign labour.

Potential increases in wages for the hi-tech jobs created by the hi-tech economy.

More jobs in the public sector ie customs and excise, border control, trade negotiators and international relations and linguistics experts

Higher interest payments from the banks on savings, this to attract more foreign investment, to this new utopia.

Overall it would seem that many of the new jobs created will be to support develop and sustain these hi-tech applications. The bulk of them will be related to administration, mainly non value added roles.

**Analysis conclusion**

The current situation i.e. 2016 Austerity almost over. The way ahead looks set fair for a prosperous, healthy, free. Peaceful and safe Europe. The potential benefits of leaving, are based heavily on conjecture and hope. Many seem to believe the UK will be making its own rules, never quite clear which rules. Or which countries will be the targets for free trade deals other than the USA.

Two world wars have been waged with an estimated 40 million ww1 and 70 to 80 million ww2 lives lost,. This driven by the vision of creating a Europe with peace security stability, prosperity and unity. Recent events could precipitate the beginning of the end of the United kingdom, with Scotland becoming independent and northern Ireland amalgamated with the south. Whilst potentially ringing the death knell on the total destruction of the European project. A visit to the D day memorial museum and the war graves in Normandy can help bring this into sharp focus, this along with many other similar sites across Europe Ypres, Verdun, Arnhem, the Somme etc, particularly when considering the sight of thousands of graves with 17, 18, 19 and 20 year old soldiers buried there. This begs the question, why are they here? Whilst remembering;

"For our today they gave their tomorrow"

We need Europe both politically and economically, the powers of the old order along with the emergent and re-emergent power blocks of the new order. Will likely present many challenges to a small island jus off the European continent. Should the United kingdom remain intact but outside the European union it is still likely that it will slip from its esteemed position of 5$^{th}$ in the world ranking of

GDP (gross domestic product) to 7$^{th}$ behind France and India, should Scotland become independent then 8$^{th}$ place  behind Canada or worse could be highly likely. Deals with USA? We don't like other people's rules perhaps Mr Trump will dance to our tune. With little or no say in the world order of rule making perhaps the likes of China , USA, the EU and the emergent economies will be compliant to our wishes? Or more likely we will become rule takers with no input to either their formulation or context.

Many will cite the 17 million that voted to leave the EU as being a significant majority and that those who question this are at best undermining democracy. With hard line Brexiteers suggesting the challenging remainers are traitors.  This begs the question should the 17 million determine the future of the 66 million (the population of the UK?) Or are some of us misguided in our belief in democracy, and begs the question, who are the real traitors?

**The following comment added June 2019**

How can anyone watching the 75$^{th}$ D day anniversary commemorations in 2019 fail to believe in the potential of unity within Europe?

It was a unity of nations that won this war, now let this unity win the peace.

## Chapter 3
## Theresa's time

Boris Johnson had successfully led the Brexit campaign against David Cameron, the then prime minister and propagator of the remain campaign. Most pundits and the polls were predicting a remain win, so arguably totally against the odds Boris had pulled of an amazing coup. None of the lies emblazoned on Boris's bus, or his inability to give a reasoned answer to any challenging or probing questions, seemed to detract the electorate. His endless rhetoric about taking back control, lost sovereignty and those nasty bureaucratic Europeans is what apparently engaged the voters.

David Cameron didn't invoke article 50 as promised if the Brexit vote was successful, but tendered his resignation, thereby initiating a leadership election within the conservative party. Interestingly Boris Johnson did not put himself forward as a candidate, maybe he knew the chalice was poisonous. Seems odd following such a great victory, and with an apparently overwhelming popularity that he would want someone else lead the conservatives at such a momentous time in the United kingdom's history. Perhaps he had anticipated the complexity of issues, conflicting interests, divisive and devious activities across the parties, along with the chancers and charlatans within his own ranks, and thus seeing David Cameron's predecessor as potential canon fodder for his own ends.

Theresa May emerged triumphant taking office 13th July 2016. It wasn't until March 29th 2017 that article 50 was invoked, marking the beginning of and a commitment to deliver the results of the EU referendum. Some early progress was evident, but before long the potential problems were identified. The Irish border, Scottish independence, the customs union and of course the so called "divorce bill", arguably all potentially foreseen problems.

Although the Scottish people had a referendum in 2014, Scottish nationalists were citing the results EU referendum as grounds for a rethink on this issue. As Scotland had clearly demonstrated a wish to remain in the EU, as did Northern Ireland. With countless agendas within parliament, Theresa was finding difficulty getting sufficient support to gain progress. Whilst holding a theoretical majority in the house, when subdivided into the various factions, there was virtually no majority for anything.

Labour at this point did not seem to have a coherent policy, seemingly not wishing to offend the remain element of the party or indeed those of the electorate that put their weight behind the leave lobby. This presenting Prime Minister May with something of a dilemma!

**Northern Ireland**
The Northern Ireland Assembly had not sat since January 2017.

Sinn Fein have seats in Westminster, but don't take them up.

The DUP do not want any borders or restrictions to mainland UK.

**Scotland**
SNP has majority in Scottish parliament with Scotland voting to remain in EU

The SNP's raison d'etre is independence from the UK.

## Conservative party

European Research Group, hell bent on a clean break (a no deal Brexit)

Many MPs from strong remain areas resisting any form of hard Brexit.

## Labour party

Many concerned about dilution or removal of employment rights.

Although sitting on the fence and being non committal on Brexit, are in support of the customs union.

Wishes to block a no deal Brexit based on potential job losses.

## Liberal Democrats

Remain at all cost, unlikely to vote for anything that doesn't maintain a close relationship with the EU. Supportive of a new referendum, now that new facts have emerged.

## Brexit Party

No deal, is the only deal, walk away and don't pay the divorce bill.

Theresa May did try to gain some consensus, but on her terms unfortunately. So the exercise was a little like "herding cats". And probably would have been anyway, even if she had taken a more conciliatory approach.

Given all the permutations of likely votes for a given proposal, and the likelihood of still getting nothing done. Theresa May decided to play her one remaining ace card, calling a general election for 8th June 2017. Her aim, to get a mandate from the people to gain a sufficient majority to get a sensible and realistic Brexit that most would accept, and at the same time reunify the country. There is an awful lot of bad blood out there, even amongst families. It is difficult to understand how people can become so entrenched in their own views, that they become totally dismissive of any counter argument or perspective, to the point of anger or even aggressive behaviour.

The result of the election, was for Theresa a bitter disappointment, the people did not give her the mandate she was looking for. As for the UK, perhaps just one step nearer to disaster. Theresa May now needs both the DUP and the ERG to support any bill she puts forward. This is beginning to look like Boris made a very shrewd move. The situation now is, that the government led by Prime Minister Theresa May is quite likely to start losing votes in the House of Commons. Effectively the DUP have the casting vote. Can she convince them to take the conservative whip? Well Theresa tried, a very stubborn and strong lady, which would suggest also a very strong will, to reunite the country. The following summary representing her genuine attempt to get the deal across the line.

15/01/2019
Parliament voted by 432 votes to 202 to reject Mrs May's deal, that set out the terms of Britain's exit from the EU on 29th March 2019, being representative of a 220 negative vote margin.

13/03/2019
With just 16 days before the 29th March Brexit deadline. Parliament again voted down the prime minister's deal by 149 votes a smaller margin than when they rejecting it in January.

27 /03/2019

Prime minister Theresa May offered her resignation if the third meaningful vote the withdrawal bill was passed, thus handing over the second element of the negotiations to her potential successor. This as an inducement to get her deal across the line. The main bone of contention being the Irish backstop. In essence the backstop was to remain in the customs union, until such time that a trade agreement with the EU that would allow the Irish north/south border to be tariff free with no checks, stops, passport control etc. Exactly as is today. To many this seemed to be a good compromise, a soft Brexit. Unfortunately the ERG posh boys and possibly the DUP saw this as a trap to keep the UK in the customs union in perpetuity, or at least that was their reasoning. Probably the real reason was particularly the ERG and certainly the Brexit party did not want any form of soft Brexit or indeed any form of compromise. On the other hand remainers still saw an opportunity to get article 50 revoked. Hence still very polarised opinions and a consequential stalemate. Seems a pity in some ways Prime Minister Theresa May had worked hard to achieve a Brexit that could appease both sides.

29/03/2019

The bill again rejected for a third time by 344 votes to 286. A margin of 58, most of the dissenters from the conservatives in the form of Boris Johnson, the ERG and the DUP, was this an own goal or an act of sabotage?

30/03/2019

Following the continued failure of Parliament to approve the Withdrawal Agreement by 29 March, thus leaving the UK in a position where it is required to leave the EU on 12 April 2019.

10/04/2019

Last minute talks in Brussels resulted in a further extension, to 31st October 2019, with a provision to leave prior to that date, if the Withdrawal Agreement were to be passed before October. Then Brexit could occur on the first day of the following month.

22/05/2019

Today it was announced that the leaders of 70 Conservative associations had signed a petition calling for a vote of no confidence in Theresa May as leader of the Conservative party.

24/05/2019

Theresa May confirmed that she would resign as conservative party leader on 7 June, but would stay in post as prime minister until a new leader is elected. Low and behold, President Trump is visiting the UK in just over a week, just what she needed.

03/06/2019

President Trumps arrives for his state visit.

President Trump's current state visit to the UK, has already highlighted some interesting perspectives on the current political situation. President Trump's "no holds barred" approach, displaying his contempt for the mayor of London Sadeq Khan, stating that he is 'a stone cold loser'. That Boris Johnson would be a good prime minister, and that Nigel Farage should be sent in to negotiate Brexit with the EU, as well as extolling the virtues of a no deal Brexit. Not a good start.

In the meantime many thousands of the UKs population are descending upon London to display their contempt for Donald Trump and the unfolding state visit. Jeremy Corbyn in his wisdom has decided to address the masses of these demonstrations, having already declined attendance at the state banquet for the president hosted by the Queen. The situation could become interesting should Mr Corbyn become prime minister in the near future; it would seem President Trump tends to demonstrate a high intolerance to dissidents of his cause. Not much help when President Trump has already stated that he would expect the NHS to be on the table in any trade deal negotiations.

Does President Trump have an agenda for the EU? Some suggest he and other Americans would like to see the EU completely disaggregated, placing the resultant smaller parts at the behest of the USA. Currently the GDP of both entities run virtually concurrently at circa 19 trillion us$ followed by China at 13$ trillion usd, and closing ground on both the EU and the USA, at about a trillion a year.

President Trump has already precipitated a trade war with China although it can be said this is a reasonable thing to do in light of the considerable imbalances in China's favour with trade as well as the intellectual property theft issues. President Trump is a nationalist who is prepared to do anything in order to maintain the status quo of USA at the top. Any trade deal with the USA for an independent UK, is about "making America great again" not about bestowing greatness in the fortunes of the UK or the potentially disunited Britain.

05/06/2019

President Trump has now visited Ireland (Eire) where he demonstrated his diplomatic credentials again by juxtaposing the Irish border problem, with that of the Mexico /USA border, where he wants to build a coast to coast wall. Clearly showing his understanding of the Good Friday agreement, the proposed backstop arrangements and the political history associated with the so called "troubles".

Mr Trump's criticism of Sadeq Khan is based around the increase In knife crime in the UK capital, perhaps president Trump should take a look at the murder rate in New York along with the increased incidence gun crime and mass murders particularly in schools.

09/06/2019

Within Belfast and Londonderry as well as several other parts of northern Ireland, there still exists many so called "peace walls" which were built to keep catholic and protestant communities apart, and indeed still do to some extent to this day. When asking the question of locals in Belfast, why have they not been removed since the Good Friday agreement, the broad answer it would seem is "because it works". So maybe there is some credibility to president Trump's thinking after all! However further questioning of local people's views suggest a strong will from both sides for the ultimate removal of these entities, but would require a considerable leap of faith and commitment from all concerned. Walls only serve to keep people apart, bridges however bring us all together.

Membership of the EU for both Eire and the UK has provided a considerable catalyst towards an acceptable unity between the "two countries". This has facilitated removal of all border controls and indeed any physical evidence of the same. Coupled to this neither Eire or the UK have signed up to the Schengen agreement as such this means the Eire border with the rest of the world shares the same fundamental features as that of the UK e.g. an appropriate passport/Visa is required for entry. Thus providing effective protection against illegal emigration.

A no deal Brexit would considerably compromise the current status quo. No one wants to be the villain of the peace by installing border controls along a 300 mile border. This in practical terms needs to be effective,  given that based  on WTO tariffs charges could range from 0 to 50% with an average of around 10% transferring from North to South and vice versa. For example Welsh farmers export a considerable amount of lamb meat to Eire. This under WTO rules attracts a two part tariff one based on price the second on weight this would equate to a tariff of around 45% dependent on the quality of the meat. This coupled to a similar circumstance when Irish beef is exported to Wales, England or Scotland. Complex isn't it! A breeding ground for bureaucracy, even without considering Barriers and quotas. The psychological aspects of a border has the potential to completely  unravel all the good will emergent from the Good  Friday agreement, removing the catalyst for unity provided by joint membership of the European Union as discussed in the previous chapter

10/06/2019

A little time for reflection based on the Peterborough by-election, which in the current situation is seen as something of a bell-weather for any general election that may occur in the near future. The previous incumbent being a labour MP, disgraced for apparently lying to a court of law.

First we had the referendum, an **"<u>overwhelming majority</u>"** of 37% to 35% to leave the EU

A 2% difference

Then a general election called by Theresa May to get a mandate from the British people to implement Brexit.

The British people took away her majority leaving her dependent on the DUP to pass legislation.

Then we had the Peterborough by-election a hinge pin of how the British people were thinking.

Labour won by a **"<u>very small margin</u>"** 31% to 29% for the Brexit Party.

A 2% difference

Interesting to see how 2% can be presented in differing ways.

Now we are in so much trouble, we need a new Prime minister. The best majority of 124,000 conservative party members will decide who this is going to be!

Wonderful thing this democracy no wonder the British people are confused.

20/06/2019
Iran has shot down an American surveillance drone, with a ground to air missile in the Strait of Hormuz. Donald Trump has tweeted as he does, "the Iranians have made a big mistake". With Boris in the frame for the PM's job, Brexit is the least of our worries, with two gung ho yanks at helm!

22/06/2019
Mr Trump has done something "sensible"! He has called off an attack on Iran at the 11th hour which purportedly, could have killed around 150 Iranians. Citing his reasons for the change of heart, he describes this response to the shooting down of the American drone as disproportionate, perhaps a glimmer of hope!

Meanwhile the other clown has won through to the final round of the "conservative's election" for the next Prime minister. Unfortunately however he seems to have engaged in an altercation with his girlfriend, to which the police were called. If the conservative electorate judge him by his domestic performance relating to commitment, loyalty, consideration for others and truthfulness, then one would expect that the more professional, calm, informed and well presented Jeremy Hunt should win, but who knows it seems everyone likes a fool who laughs at his own gaffes, probably if Mr Bean were standing it could be a landslide victory.

23/06/2019

Boris Johnson says attitudes have changed since the negotiations with the EU, and he fully expects to be able to do a deal by October. Boris goes on to say "the EU can't wait to get their hands on the £39 billion divorce settlement". Suggesting he is ready to pay it, despite his previous descent when it was part of Theresa May's deal with the EU.

09/07/2019

Boris Johnson on the hustings was questioned relating to UK ambassador Sir Kim Durrock in USA and his refusal to give his support. President Trump had requested the British government to remove Sir Kim Durrock from his post of ambassador, on the grounds that he had made derogatory comments about him. This was not denied, but the said comments were not made in public and put forward a reasoned perspective of the American president. They were in fact leaked from a memo to the British government, and should have been totally confidential. Was it that Boris had no wish offend the President Trump. Of course we will be making our own rules following exiting the EU, won't we, and certainly not responding to the whims of Donald Trump. So perhaps a good time to make a stand.

16/07/2019

Boris's kipper from the Isle of Man, he stated EU bureaucracy dictated that, to send kippers in the post they would need to be accompanied with an ice pack. Which in the opinion of the Isle man fish processors was totally unnecessary, and the plastic used to contain the ice was also a threat to the environment. Boris explained they had been sending them for years without any problem, then the EU interfered with their ludicrous rules.

Unfortunately Boris didn't seem to know that the Isle of Man is not a member of the EU and the rule was made by the UK government. Whoops!!

18/07/2019

Mr Trump's "send them back" jibes and the ensuing rally with the crowd chanting "SEND HER BACK" repeatedly. resembled the Nuremburg rallies of

1936 , but without the nazi salute. This in a north Carolina rally and directed at Ilhan Omar a Minnesota Democrat. Perhaps that would have made him feel back home, given his Germanic background. He seems to forget that if all the $1^{st}$ $2^{nd}$ and $3^{rd}$ generation "Americans" went back to where they came from, then there wouldn't be many people left in the USA, apart from the native Indians that have been trampled into insignificance.

21/07/2019

It looks like Boris Johnson is going to be Prime Minister, Philip Hammond has announced his resignation as chancellor of the exchequer, thus one less voice of reason. So with Johnson and Trump at the helm this could potentially exacerbate a predictable outbreak of coulrophobia.

# Chapter 4

## Boris's Time to Brexit day

24/07/2019

Well Boris Johnson has it, he is now Prime Minister. Question is can this "captain Jack sparrow character" actually fix it, if you watch pirates of the Caribbean films then he probably can!! So now the Americans have one foot in the door (Boris was born in New York) and president Trump likes him. I suppose one could say two clowns in a circus are better than one. The chlorinated chicken and hormone fed beef from the USA will be at bargain prices, and the Welsh will be delighted with 40 plus percent tariffs their lamb attracts on the EU markets.

Wonderful acceptance speech by Boris, sounds like he can change the world with his "plans", wonder why he didn't stand for prime minister 3 years ago and save the hard working British people all the agony and uncertainty of the last 3 years and 3 months. With Boris it's a done deal. Goodbye food banks and austerity. Everyone will be buying British, wages will soar, crime will drop and Great Britain will be the envy of the World. At last the utopia the British people deserve. Boris's "master plan" has been 3 years in the making and will be implemented in three months, should be amazing. Watch this space.

28/07/2019

Perhaps Boris is not so much a clown, more a puppet? Reference to the ERG and Dominic Cummings, puppeteers incorporated.

Boris has his technological solutions to the invisible border in Northern Ireland, to which he has not explained in practical terms as yet. He has spoken of movement of goods, but not yet of people and their freedom of movement, maybe he plans to have all foreigners tattooed with a barcode that invisible cameras will read at the borders.

Pretty Patel is the new Home Secretary, perhaps she would benefit from some guidance on immigration from Nigel Farage and Boris Johnson's big friend, President Trump.

29/07/2019

Today the pound hit a new low the spot rate is now 91 pence for 1 euro, the rate 31/05/2016 was 76 pence. Ie the pound is worth 19.7 percent less now than it was following the referendum vote. The USD 68 pence and 82 respectively equating to a 20.7

percent drop in the value of the pound. Does this suggest that international markets have got it wrong with Brexit? Although do Boris and his puppeteers have some doubts because some them seem to be moving their investments out of this country i.e. sir James Dyson, Jacob Rees-mogg, Tim Martin (Wetherspoons), Farage and co.

30/07/2019

Why is so much effort going into a no deal Brexit, perhaps the no deal has always been the planned objective of the ERG. They want a northern style Hong Kong, for the UK. A UK devoid of employment law and regulation. Where the masses do as they are told, work in sweat shops and are grateful for their place in life.

04/08/2019

This week once again president Trump takes a swipe at Sadiq Khan, seems to have an overwhelming obsession with him, almost like a man with a vendetta. Ironically and sadly his comments have once again been followed by a mass gun incidents in the USA, 20 plus dead in El Paso, and 9 plus dead in Daytona. Incidentally El Paso would seem to be someone with leanings towards president Trump ie white Popularist nationalist views. Perhaps Mr Trump should concern himself with his own problems and not those of the Mayor of London, who himself is trying to battle with popularist nationalism and an emergent culture of anarchy and vigilantism.

11days gone Prime Minister Johnson has now visited Wales, Scotland and Ireland, throwing money that he doesn't have, at everything that enhances his populKarist perspective. Will he visit Brussels? Or does he already know the answer? Or perhaps the answer doesn't matter, because his true agenda is a no deal Brexit, in line with the ERG and Nigel Farage. God help us!!

**Time for personal reflection perhaps.**

Feeling at this moment in time that my perspective seems altogether more biased than ever before against Brexit. Whilst being even more strongly pro unity and integrity of UK, the European union, the United nations and indeed the unity of the human race. Finding the rise of popularist nationalism quite frightening, not so much for older generations, but for our children and grandchildren. The key concerns being that popularist nationalism can precipitate anarchy and vigilantism and ultimately tribalism.

So with this mind I am reflecting on my own life and the influences on that life in terms of health, education, employment and opportunities.

Born in 1947 in small town in Huntingdonshire, in a two up two down rented house, no maternity hospitals those days. The NHS (National Health Service) like me had just been born. My mother was a housewife and my father a driver for a furniture removal company. Married women of that time did not work unless they were in a professional role such as a teacher, accountant, doctor etc. Following bouts of flooding, our family were moved to one of the "new new council houses" many thousands of them were built across the country, in part to replace housing stock as replacements for those destroyed by war, As well as providing employment for those returning from the war. This new house not only had electricity, it had an inside lavvy and a bathroom. My schooling was the standard state schooling of the time. My first obstacle was the 11plus exam, which unfortunately I failed. Dad was devastated particularly as he had passed his 11 plus, but my grandparents could not afford to let him go to grammar school. By reason of the cost of uniform, transport, sports equipment etc. So upset by this dad went to see headmaster looking for reasons as to why I fell short of the required standards. Apparently he said that I "didn't have a propensity towards academia" and that if I worked hard at the new Secondary Modern school, I might get in at the technical college and even get a skilled job, by following an apprenticeship of some sort. Dad warmed to the idea, mainly because in the intervening years he had enrolled on a postal course and gained a city and guilds in radio engineering. This provided the opportunity to switch from lorry driving to a job with a local radio and television retailer on the Repair and installation side of the business.

The Secondary Modern was great, only been open for one year, the science labs were amazing. The old Headmaster turned out to be right! With an apprenticeship materialising along with a sandwich course at the local Technical College. It has been a very good life since, despite the UK joining the so called Common Market, which ultimately evolved into the European Union. (see p. 9) my reflective statement to an interviewee. Ah "that feels better" we should never lose sight of where we came from!

10/08/2019

GDP figures released showing a contraction in the economy of 0.2%, some would say a somewhat marginal decline. Which in essence is true, when measured in pounds sterling. However when measured against the major world currencies ie the USD and the Euro then the combined decline in currency over the last 12 months would be enough the take the UK from $5^{th}$ place in the world "pecking order" to $7^{th}$ behind France and India. New figures also show a increase in unemployment, but with an overall increase in wages paid. Given these and other emergent trends this could represent the top of the roller-coaster. Potentially unemployment will further increase, along with inflation, the pound could slip to parity with the euro or less, the stock market falling below the 7000 level on the FTSE 100 index. This considerably exacerbated by the very high risks associated with a no deal Brexit.

18/08/2019

Another leaked document from the government, spreading doom and gloom on a no deal Brexit. Are these people scaremongers or realists? Boris Johnson claims these are attempts from pro Europeans to undermine his negotiating position, but to date no sign of any negotiations. Are the British public being tricked into just what the ERG want, a no deal Brexit. This with total disregard the unity and continuity of the United kingdom, the sustainability of the Good Friday agreement, the impact on foreign exchange or potential hardship to a considerable majority of the population.

20/08/2019

A lovely quote today, "sometimes doing nothing is the best way to make progress" (Alan, viking cruise19). So why are we actually leaving the EU? Will we all be more; prosperous, healthy, educated, safe. At the moment it is not looking too good, holidays and purchases abroad are on average 20% more expensive than 3 years ago even when discounting inflation currently circa 2% per annum. So perhaps some things are best left as they are!!

23/08/19

Boris Johnson seems quite upbeat about the potential for a new deal relating to the back stop, both Angela Merkel and Emmanuel Macron have suggested that they will certainly look at any plan that Boris may present, but at this moment Boris and his team seem completely devoid of any reasoned arguments or any substantive plan or reasoned arguments. Or is he just setting the to blame the EU for the failure of an acceptable deal. The ERG and its followers do not want a deal, they want the pound to fall further, making the so called hard working people of the country even poorer in international terms, reducing their employment rights, to give them much more control over the masses. This enabling a bargain basement approach to buying back British investment on the cheap. Companies like lidl and Aldi will have much more buying power than the likes of Tesco, Morrison, Sainsbury, etc. Buying goods with the strong Euro, enabling a potential to undercut their British competitors on their own high street.

On the northern Ireland backstop question open borders with wildly differing tariffs i.e. WTO and EU tariffs would create a haven for smugglers, grey and black market trading as well as fraudsters

25/08/19

Donald Trump hails Boris Johnson as "the right man to deliver Brexit" (daily mail). He certainty is the right man for Donald Trump, the break-up of the EU would suit his power game just fine. This well known strategy of "divide and conquer" seems to be working quite well at the moment. Currently the GDP of the USA and the EU are virtually in parity at around 21 trillion usd. In the event of Brexit, then the EU would fall short of the USA by around 2.8 trillion. Mr Trump is suggesting a good deal with the UK, very nice, but Mr Trump's definition of a good deal is, a good deal for the USA. With his Popularist Nationalistic approach just consider the way he treated fellow members of NAFTA recently, in particular Mexico (my deal or no deal).

Boris has taken hard line with Donald Trump telling him that, the refusal of the USA to take our pork pies, and shower trays is not acceptable and the NHS is definitely off limits. It is unlikely that Boris Johnson would have any idea what it is like to find a local NHS dentist, or for aged people some of whom require regular ear syringing to get this service on the NHS without waiting for 3 months for an appointment. The health service is systematically being dismantled, don't be surprised if Trump's USA does not move in on these peripheral spin offs to take the NHS by attrition. Of course we can all be sure that Boris Johnson won't be taking chlorine washed chicken, or hormone fed beef as part of the deal.

The likely outcome is that Boris with his sympathetic droopy puppy dog eyes and floppy unkempt hair, will become just a cute little lap dog to Donald Trump. The man that separates children from their parents as a deterrent to would be immigrants.

28/08/19

Boris has now prorogued parliament, but he said he wasn't going to do that. Must have been just another misunderstanding. It would seem this is another step towards a contrived no deal Brexit, goodbye Good Friday agreement. What next for the Irish problem, all the blood spilled on both sides of the divide, the progress that has made in the last almost 20 years since its inception this in terms of the reduction of Barriers and freedom of movement between north and south. Boris's technological solutions may have some credence with goods, if the powers that be ignore the booze and fag runs, but what of services and people? Will people need a passport to travel from England to Northern Ireland and vice versa? Perhaps facial recognition would help, or tattooed barcode, but then by definition there is a barrier, but nevertheless a boundary/border. Europe has been the key catalyst towards the current peace and reconciliation that has taken place. How many British servicemen lost their lives or still carry the scares of trying to bring about this fragile peace. These service personnel are still paying the price, where consecutive governments have failed to draw a line under the events of the so called "troubles" a moratorium for all not just those considered as terrorists.

02/09/19

Never trust a clown, what you see is not what you get. Herr Johnson's latest actions, would tend to support this notion. Threatening to sack Conservative ministers who do not fully support him, as well as removing other Conservative MPs from the whip and getting them deselected should there be a general election. Herr Johnson is a "mean poker player" the odds are very close particularly with a virtually non electable Labour party with Mr Corbyn at the helm. Perhaps a switch to kier Starmer could change Labour's fortunes? It would seem that Herr Johnson is planning to; run the clock down to achieve a no deal Brexit "by accident", or to throw the opposition parties into turmoil in order to call a general election, subsequently and potentially achieving a win with his loyal Tories in cahoots with the Brexit party. A party that would now seem to have some considerable momentum! Meanwhile Boris Johnson continues to suggest the "no deal Brexit" option is merely a negotiation ploy to shock the unrelenting EU into removing the backstop.

03/09/19

Johnson's speech outside no.10 yesterday, which many thought would be the precursor to a general election. Instead it was a veiled threat relating to a failure of parliament to support his otherwise unspecified approach to getting a deal with the EU, underpinned with some conjecture

This is a very worrying time with the ERG (European Research Group) wielding very great power well beyond their democratic remit. The ERG consists of 54 subscribers in the form of conservative members of parliament some of whom are members of the government. The term European seems to relate to an obsession with the European project and its demise, the research element does not provide balanced perspectives, but seeks out that which apparently undermines the project. Those strongly opposing the ERG have suggested they're a bunch of chancers and charlatans;

*"Taxpayers' money is being used to fund this influential group of hard-line pro-Brexit Conservative MPs who are increasingly operating as a "party-within-a-party". Cusick, James (8 September 2017). "MPs demand full investigation of hard-Brexit backing Tory "party within a party"". openDemocracy.*

Retrieved 18th January 2018.

*In July 2019, a tribunal declared that the ERG's research must be made public. Corderoy, Jenna; Geoghegan, Peter (2 July 2019). "Tax-funded research by Rees-Mogg's ERG must be released, tribunal rules". openDemocracy. Retrieved 2 July 2019.*

*The ERG has also been funded by a secretive group called the Constitutional Research Council. Corderoy, Jenna; Geoghegan, Peter (2 July 2019). "Tax-funded research by Rees-Mogg's ERG must be released, tribunal rules". openDemocracy.*

Retrieved 2 July 2019.

Quotes from openDemocracy an independent media platform covering world affairs.

4/09/19

Mr. Johnson now has all his scapegoats lined up, so if his plans "not yet revealed" go wrong. Then he has a scapegoat for most of the potential scenarios. If he looses the vote on removing the no deal Brexit, then it is the fault of the speaker (who Boris suggests is biased in favour of remainers) the rebels within the conservative party and the Labour party who just want his "negotiations" to fail by hypothetically "chopping his legs off" in terms of his negotiating leverage.

If there is no movement in the position of the EU. Then it is the bad boys of Europe punishing us for wanting to leave, or because they simply don't understand Boris's alternative arrangements.

08/09/19

The irony of the current situation is, we could have left the EU on 30th March 19, but for Mr Johnson and his ERG compatriots voting against the deal which Theresa May had put together. Which was much better than the crash out which seems to be the true agenda of Boris Johnson and the ERG. As a further irony Boris Johnson voted against the Government 3 times and never was threatened with, or had the Conservative whip removed by his predecessor Theresa May, whom it is suggested accepted and respected his opinions.

10/09/19

Well parliament has now been prorogued by the "pro-rogues," what next? Will Boris get a deal with the EU now that he is not answerable to parliament, or has he just kicked the can far enough down the road so that we accidentally exit the EU without a deal! The government has covered all possible scenarios of implementing their plans, having a scapegoat for each potential disaster that may occur. The speaker for being continually biased, the leader of the SNP in parliament Ian Blackford for representing the views of the Scottish people, Jeremy Corbyn for not wanting an immediate election, the conservative rebels who voted with their conscience and not their pay packet. The Liberal Democrats for daring to suggest that remaining should be an option for the people that is based on the emergent truths. The French and Germans who are committed to the European project, or the EU itself who are still waiting for his new proposals.

Boris says he will not ask for a delay in the Brexit date, he says he *"would rather be dead in a ditch"* proof that he does have some good ideas. Boris Johnson it seems sees himself as an eagle surrounded by turkeys. Boris has always struggled with ornithology, as he does not appear to know the difference between turkeys and eagles, indeed birds of any type would not seem to be his forte.

11/11/119

The Scottish court of appeal has now ruled the prorogation of parliament is unlawful. This of course is all the Remainers fault. What do these people think they are doing, here's Boris Johnson trying to run a legitimate dictatorship and these narrow minded Remainers seem to be undermining him at every turn. Wonder what trick or slight of hand Dominic Cummings will provide next?

Boris Johnson of course does not tell lies, he does however seem to have an innate propensity to mislead, or be misunderstood.

14/09/19

David Cameron reveals his memoirs, making devastating attacks on Boris Johnson and Michael Gove. Suggesting they wrecked his Government, by *"leaving the truth at home"* in their campaign for Brexit.

16/09/19

Boris Johnson had a meeting with Xavier Bettel Prime Minister of Luxembourg, Boris failed to attend the arranged press conference following their meeting on the grounds that the crowd were too noisy. However Xavier Bettel went on to address the journalists without our dear Boris, who it seems only has his interests of "prospective voters" at heart. Mr Brettel told the gathered press representatives that Mr Johnson had not yet put forward any plan of substance, merely presenting verbal conjecture, with no supporting documentary evidence of how this could work. But yet again we only have the word of a vindictive Europhile. Boris will soon correct this misalignment of views, presenting his well constructed and considered plans of 3 years in the making. All ready for dotting the i's and crossing the t's prior to presentation to European leaders ahead of the EU summit (consilium), now just 1 month away. How can anyone believe this is unachievable, given that Boris is in charge.

In the meantime Jo Swinson, leader of the Liberal Democrats has suggested that they should adopt a policy of revoking article 50 on day one, should the

Liberal Democrats be elected in any forthcoming general election. This without another referendum potentially based on reality and truth as many have suggested. Which it can be said is totally wrong and undemocratic showing no respect for the leave result in the referendum. Whilst others would suggest the referendum was built on a tissue of lies, such as the figures on Boris's bus, Gove's implications of being flooded with Turkish emigrants etc. The fact remains that 37% is not a majority just 2% more than 35%. So was the referendum itself democratic? Jo Swinson's polarised perspective could be seen as being totally democratic and unambiguous, particularly for those voters with Brexit at the top of their agenda. The Brexiteers wanting an unequivocal total break from the EU be able to invoke their democratic right by voting for the Brexit party. The pro-European remainers will have no doubt about what they are voting for, should they choose a Liberal Democrat candidate or indeed a Scottish National Party candidate. This polarisation may provide clear water between parties, but as far as the Liberal Democrats are concerned this is a very high risk strategy. As such this could potentially become Swinson's swansong.

In the meantime it is likely that the Labour party will engage some alignment between the factions of it's own party as opposed to sitting on the fence, trying be all things to all people. This prior to a likely general election which will likely be either in the next couple of months or early in the new year. The conservatives however are likely to haemorrhage more members to other parties, this further reducing its influence and power within parliament, whilst initiating more power to the ERG within the conservative party. Could this be the catalyst for a liaison between the conservatives and the Brexit party?

19/09/19

The Supreme Court of the UK concluded today having heard all the evidence relating to the prorougation of parliament. The verdict as to whether this was legal or otherwise will be delivered early next week. Should this prorougation be found illegal, will Boris Johnson take his appeal to the European Court of Justice!! Just a thought.

20/09/19

The government has in recent days released some outline plans to the EU negotiating team, which it would seem have been met with a degree of optimism. Will this be the breakthrough we have all been waiting for, or is this just a precursor to a Theresa May mark 4?

21/09/19

It would seem that Boris's plans have about the same substance and meaning as the writing on his campaign bus, or his kipper prank.

23/09/19

The labour party conference today failed, to state the party's position on Brexit, it would seem to be pursuing a "neutral line" somewhat as before. Some would describe this stance as "sitting on the fence", trying to be all things to all people. Going back three years to the referendum, although labour's policy was at that time to remain in the EU. Jeremy Corbyn never seemed to respect this Labour policy and it could be said that his intransigence caused the loss of the referendum to the Brexiteers. Jeremy Corbyn has the illusion that somehow, the EU will succumb to his negotiating skills, by offering a far superior deal than that previously proffered to either Theresa May, or to Boris Johnson if indeed he ever gets one. Basically it would seem that Jeremy

Corbyn wants to win a general election first then, negotiate a deal, then decide labour's policy followed by a new referendum. This would consist of a choice between Jeremy Corbyn's deal or remain in the EU.

24/09/19

Today is the day relating to the prorougation of parliament, everything hanging on the findings of the high court, what will be the next twist or turn in this saga. The prorougation of parliament has been deemed unlawful. Will Boris appeal to the ECJ European Court of Justice, how ironic would that be!! Thank goodness the law has protected us from this bunch of scheming vagabonds, i.e. Boris Johnson the very smug Jacob Rees-Mogg and the cronies of the so called ERG (European Research Group) or as described by Shami Chakrabarti as *"Boris Johnson and his arrogant privileged chums."*

Boris does not agree with the Supreme Court decision even though it was a unanimous verdict, eleven to none. Whilst his supporters suggest this is all a conspiracy, perpetrated by remainers to undermine his authority and stop Brexit. How many more lies or contrived misunderstandings does he need to engage with, before his advocates stop trusting him?

Parliament resumes tomorrow, will this be the equivalent of "gun fight at the OK coral" or perhaps "Custer's last stand"

As a result of Parliament reconvening tomorrow, Jeremy Corbyn delivered his closing speech for the Labour party conference today, very charged and dynamic, probably Jeremy Corbyn at his best. Typically an electioneering speech everyone is going to get something; pensioners, students, education, NHS, infrastructure and yes everything that is not bolted down will be nationalised, as one might expect from someone of Jeremy Corbyn's ilk.

Whilst still appearing to be sitting on the fence with Brexit, coming from Jeremy himself the position seems a little more clear. His negotiated deal included a customs union with the EU, which could potentially resolve the Irish problem and gain acceptance with the EU. This and other elements of his plan, could make for a softer version of the Theresa May plan and perhaps provide a good compromise between Brexiteers and Remainers. So maybe his apparent sitting on the fence could be more about unity than indecision.

25/09/19

Jacob Rees-Mogg opens the batting today, suggesting that the Supreme Court judgment is "tantamount to a constitutional coup" anyone could be forgiven for thinking he was talking about the prorogation of parliament for an unprecedented length of time. The Brexit camp in general seem to consider the Supreme Court's verdict to be wrong and undemocratic, whilst resenting the judiciary's interference in politics which they say is beyond the remit of the Supreme Court, even if it is deemed that the prime minister has broken the law. Boris continues to pitch his people versus parliament line, suggesting the traitors are going against the will of the people, referencing the 17 million people that voted to leave the EU. Perhaps he conveniently forgets to mention the 28 million people that voted in the last general election for our current parliament. The people of parliament have been elected by the people to represent their constituent's best interests not their misinformed beliefs or whims. The elected members of parliament are in the main intelligent, well informed professional people, with a wide perspective on current affairs in general and a finger on the pulse international influences. This is democracy, not the dictatorship that Boris Johnson and his privileged posh boy friends of the so called ERG, tried to impose on the back of prorogation. So why not let the MPs do what the people elected them to do.

It is not the pro Europeans that have prevented Brexit, it is the no deal, hard-line, no compromise Brexiteers of the ERG that are trying to run the show. Back in March this year Theresa May had worked hard to achieve a deal which on the face of it seemed like a reasonable compromise. This could satisfy a broad church of opinion with an element of compromise, but no Boris Johnson, with an eye on the top job, voted against his own conservative government along with his privileged chums. Which ultimately perpetrated the resignation of Theresa May. In many people's minds this is sabotage.

Prime ministers question time, Boris was on form, no apologies relating to breaking the law just arrogant aggression. But he really took the biscuit with one of his typical gaffes. A female MP Jess Phillips, raised concern over some of the degrading language been used in parliament and how much of this was repeated on the streets frequently with added venom. She went on to say that if this were allowed to escalate, it could end with another tragedy like the murder of Jo Cox. Boris suggested the best memorial to Jo Cox was to get on with Brexit and getting it done. Jo Cox was a prolific remain campaigner, let us hope this was "Just another gaffe" Jo Cox gave her life for her beliefs. Perhaps Boris should make his apologies, or perhaps this was deliberately part of his scheme, lets hope not.

26/09/19

No apologies today, shame on Boris let's hope no one takes his dead in a ditch comments to seriously

Angela Merkel came to the aid of Condor airlines a German subsidiary of Thomas cook, with a 350 million Euro bailout. What a pity the British government could not reciprocate with help for Thomas Cook UK, this one of the longest standing and well known British companies. No doubt the nasty EU will be at fault somewhere along the line, or is it that good leaders do what's right and take the flack afterwards.

27/09/19

Dominic Cummings, yes that's the democratically unelected Dominic Cummings has once again come to the fore. He is suggesting that the threats of violence should be no surprise to those who seek to undermine the will of the British people. He even went on to suggest that further interference by remainers could precipitate violence on the streets the like of the "Gilet Jaune" in France. This is becoming more like an episode of eastenders where the biggest bullies always win. A sad day when reasoned argument is met with threats of violence and intimidation. The bottom line is the Brexiteers Cummings, Johnson, Rees-Mogg etal have run out reasoned argument and are resorting to the "do you want a smack in the mouth" approach. There are many in the opposition parties demanding Boris Johnson's resignation perhaps this should extend to his chief puppeteer Dominic Cummings.

29/09/19

The newspapers are all pursuing the improprieties of Boris Johnson and Donald Trump, two of the world's leading politicians. Trump could be impeached for abuse of his position and status, by coercing the Ukrainian president to dish some dirt on a potential USA presidential candidate. Boris could face criminal charges for misappropriation of funds when he was London mayor. If these are world leaders what are the rest up to, how many of them are criminals that just haven't been caught?

Could be a vote of no confidence in Boris Johnson this week, initiated by an alliance between Labour and the SNP. Probably doing their numbers this weekend to see if they stack up, for what some may call a coup d'état.

30/09/19
Further "mud slinging" today relating to Boris's exploits, probably precipitated by the opportunistic "me to brigade" which only serve to cloud the real issues. On a more optimistic note it is looking like the Liberal Democrats may be getting on board for setting up a temporary government of unity possibly under the leadership of Jeremy Corbyn, although alternatively the much respected Kenneth Clarke has been suggested.


01/10/19
Boris has a plan!! To be made public in two or three days, let's hope it's good, and who's going to get the blame if it isn't?

The conservative party conference seems to be the focus of the day, where we are being told the great things they are going to do post Brexit; more hospitals, more police officers on the beat, investment in infrastructure, more money into education, increases in state pensions, increases the minimum pay rates etc. Looks a little like some of the things Theresa May was planning prior to her resignation, perhaps two of the same promises are better than one. Of course these prospective offerings, are reversing what has been imposed by this conservative government over the last nine years. i.e. Cuts in police numbers, less investment in real terms in healthcare, closures of hospitals, higher costs for students in terms o increased tuition fees, coupled to higher interest rates on student loans to 6,5%, more dumbing down achievement standards in education to make the pass rates look better. They don't tell you they increased the number of food banks by about 300%. Or how claimants have to wait three to five weeks to get financial support, these people live from week to week they do not have money stashed away in foreign bank accounts. In fact they are more likely to have unpaid debts, credit cards for example. So please don't insult the British people, by insulting their intelligence with your patronising sympathetic tone.

02/10/19

29 days to go Boris is set to announce the presentation of his take it or leave it deal to the EU. It would seem that it will be a Theresa May mark 4 deal, with modifications to the backstop arrangements. Some sort of away from the border checks, so that everyone can pretend they are not really there. If the technology is all that Boris suggests it is, the likelihood is that these away from the border checkpoints will be totally unmanned. Something like an electronic honesty box, but instead of processing a few pounds/euros it will be dealing with many millions. Seems like an open invitation to all the black and grey marketeers. Just think the border could become the black market capital of the world. Even otherwise honest entrepreneurs could be tempted by the spoils.

Radio 4 this morning carried a report relating to the potential impact of a no deal Brexit on the dairy industry in Northern Ireland. The spokesman for the dairy producers, said WTO tariffs on dairy products are 40% and with profit margins of 3% then with the absence of significant subsidies from the British government, the likely outcome is stark in its inevitability. To date the government has provided little more than lip service towards subsidies.

The closing speeches of the Conservative's annual conference this lunchtime. As expected Boris Johnson  is going to put money into virtually everything the Conservatives have taken money out of in the last nine years; NHS, police, infrastructure, technology etc, and cut taxes plus raising the living wage threshold. All wonderful stuff with lots of really clever humour mainly aimed at the SNPs Nicola sturgeon and Alex Salmond, the Labour party, Jeremy Corbyn and John Bercow. Perhaps a little like a John Cleese take on the Nuremberg rallies.

03/10/19

Boris has released his plan, a little different from that which had been rumoured, probably a little early for constructive comments. On the face of it looks quite complex in nature, but looks like the main weakness may be the potentially open door to smugglers and illicit traders.

An interesting coincidence that Donald Trump has just won a case against the EU relating to historic subsidies made to Airbus. As such he will apply tariffs to European goods amounting to around 5 billion Euros, this including products such as scotch whisky. Trump of course would dearly like the British people to leave the EU, not because he is just itching to do a trade deal with the UK which only has an economy about 12% the GDP of the USA. He sees an opportunity to put a "nail in the coffin" of the EU, fitting with the agenda of Trump and his associates, this to bring about the demise of the EU. Thereby reinstating USA into an undisputed position as the "world's top dog" economy.

Back on Boris his new offering to the EU would seem quite convoluted and ambiguous. Two sets of customs arrangements between two different countries, with border checks that don't don't exist but do. The Northern Ireland assembly or Stormont as it is frequently called has a vote on it, every four years related to its content and application along with a unilateral veto on its continuation. Stormont has not met for the last two years, coupled to the likelihood that if this "deal" is accepted, it won't meet for the next three years given Sinn Fein's current position. Let's see what the politicians make of it. Rest assured if this "excuse for a solution" fails it won't be Boris and his government's fault. They have a scapegoat no doubt for every conceivable outcome, even winning, if that goes wrong. Winning for Boris Johnson would be a clean no deal Brexit, that is his and his ERG compatriots true agenda, the rest his just smoke and mirrors.

04/10/19

Various posturing moves by various conservatives, mainly from Boris and co, the DUP and ERG. Whilst the Labour party, SNP and Liberal Democrats are generally fairly quiet, apart from restating their current position. Clearly waiting to what happens next.

05/10/19

A new liberal Democrat member has emerged in the form of Heidi Allen from the Change party. It would seem that Dominic Grieve an ex-conservative party member, will not have a liberal Democrat running against him should he stand to be re-elected in any forthcoming parliamentary election.

06/10/19

Some first class negotiating skills demonstrated by Boris "take it or leave it" Johnson, once again. Now he is threatening to sabotage by veto, the every day business of the EU, should they grant a further extension. As well as potentially engaging the services of Nigel Farage potentially sending him

Brussels to throw "brick bats into the EU pond". This should create a good atmosphere for meaningful negotiations. In fairness to Boris there is no ambiguity in what he is staying here. Nigel Farage has an excellent and extensive record of criticism and sabotage of anything related to the European project.

Amid much criticism of the Lisbon treaty inclusions coming into force during 2020, of which are to; remove the single state veto, along with no abstentions when voting, coupled to a majority voting system based on the gravity of the proposal. For example to change the import tariff on bananas would require a simple majority i.e. 51% plus. To change the constitution of the EU would require a 75% plus majority, this is currently 100%. Thus effectively removing any veto. Unfortunately this implementation will be too late to stop Boris Johnson and co causing disruptions to EU parliamentary business. Although this may help in the future if Brexit materialises and the trade negotiations commence. This potentially could lead to a better deal for the UK requiring only 75% of the EU membership to accept the final proposals, as opposed to currently with the Withdrawal Agreement, where 100% acceptance is required.

08/10/19

Boris Johnson seems to have conceded that a Brexit deal is not a realistic possibility, is anyone realistically surprised, Boris is playing the end game. What has happened is this is all part of his original agenda? Meanwhile back in parliament Michael Gove is delivering prime minister's question time, and is suggesting that there is still "light at the end of the tunnel" with an opportunity for a good deal, perhaps they both follow different media sources.

Parliament prorogued again, but only for three days. Parliament will be reconvened on Monday 14th October following the Queen's speech.

09/10/19

A little worrying this morning from an economics perspective, with 3 key factors reported; Industrial output was down again this month, the pound lost value yesterday and the stock market also dipped. Could we be heading for a recession? No doubt anyone bold enough to support that assertion would be branded a traitor and scaremonger. Part of the reasoning behind this assertion is based on historic patterns, in that when the pound goes up, the stock market goes down and vice versa, a seesaw effect, this coupled to the low industrial output and two consecutive quarters of only just positive growth figures.

Donald Trump rears his head again with Turkish forces invading northern Syria following the removal of some the American military presence there. President Trump had already threatened consequences if Turkey launched any attacks on the Kurdish people, those who had played a considerable role in defeating ISIS in that area of Syria. The Kurdish people are seen as terrorists to the Turks and friends and allies to the Americans. Trump said that he would "bust the Turkish economy". The Kurds had warned of this, but seemed to fall on deaf ears, precipitating the comment "the Kurds didn't help us in Normandy".

Another topical issue relating to president Trump's intransigence, a teenage motorcyclist Harry Dunn was knocked down and killed by the wife of an American diplomat, whilst driving her car from an American intelligence complex in Northamptonshire. Following the incident she had offered full cooperation with the British police in investigating the incident. She subsequently claimed diplomatic immunity, returning to the United states. Boris Johnson followed this with a request to President Trump, that she should return to assist with enquiries. This request was declined, apparently without reason. Seems President Trump is a good friend when he has something to gain from the relationship. With those sort of friends you don't need enemies.

13/10/19

Tomorrow the Queen will reopen parliament. In the meantime Boris is suggesting there is a light at the end of the tunnel, intimating that a deal may be on the cards. As such he has convened a parliamentary meeting on Saturday 19th October, significantly this follows an EU council summit commencing on 17th October for two days. Overall this week the key players in this ongoing saga, have been relatively tight lipped. Although Nicola Sturgeon and Ian Blackwell, have been raising the stakes on Scottish independence as well as a vote of no confidence in Boris Johnson. Ken Clarke (father of the house) says the thought of being prime minister in an interim government, would make for an interesting end to his career, perhaps just to let everyone know that he is, up for the job!

14/10/19

This potentially could be a week for the history books; Parliament is reopened, the European Council meets on Thursday, an extraordinary meeting of parliament has been convened for Saturday, Nicola Sturgeon has given notice that a new independence referendum is definitely on the agenda, President Trump is pulling out the remaining USA forces in northern Syria. Meanwhile Boris Johnson is still seeking the switch for the light at the end of the tunnel. Those of a more cynical disposition still believe he isn't really looking.

Observers of this narrative may consider there to be an unreasonable emphasis on the antics of Donald Trump! The reality is, a no deal Brexit would mean that a comprehensive trade deal with the USA would become critical to the well being of the UK, particularly in the short and medium term. What pound of flesh would Trump have his sights on? Perhaps something related to the further demise of the European project. Trump's agenda is to make the USA great again, not that it wasn't in most people's eyes. Nevertheless his agenda exists and he cares not for friends or the environment, they are viewed merely as collateral damage.

In essence those not liking some of the rules emanating from the EU, might be a little disappointed with the empathy received to any resistance of acceptance of the likely terms and conditions imposed by the Trump regime.

15/10/19

Nicola Sturgeon threw a spanner in the works today, in her closing speech at the SNP's national conference. She announced the party's intention to engage with the protocol to enable a Scottish independence referendum in 2020.

Michel Barnier didn't help either suggesting that the deadline for Boris's proposed plan is midnight tonight, ready for the European Council conference on 17-18th October. Making for a very interesting day tomorrow.

16/10/19

Fifteen days to go, talks with EU negotiators went on until almost 1-30 am this morning. Suggestions are that a deal is on the cusp, but the detail may take a little longer, pundits indicating that two or three months may be required for legal and technical details, this based on comments from Mrs Merkel and Mr Macron.

Michel Barnier's deadline has passed, the wire has been stretched, some degree of optimism from peripheral players, but no light at the end of the tunnel at 8 pm this evening. News just accessed from the Daily Mail, suggests the planned deal has been "scuppered by the DUP". Likely more details will emerge over the next couple of days.

Just to add insult to injury President Trump will be imposing a 25% tariff on Scotch whiskey and Kashmir woollen products in the next few days. It's good to have a special relationship just when you really need it!

17/10/19

Boris's deal looks a little like a Theresa May mark 2; moving the Northern/Southern Irish border to the Irish sea, and for continuation of alignment with the EU customs union, that needs an ongoing consent vote from Stormont. Stormont incidentally has not sat for three years! Indeed if they did it needs to be recognised that northern Ireland voted to remain in the EU. So if they were to sit again, it is unlikely that the consent would be removed. Quite clearly the DUP who, coincidentally did not vote for the Good Friday agreement would regard this deal as step towards the reunification of Ireland. As well as this the Scottish people who also voted to remain in the EU, could argue that they also want to remain in the customs union! Could this precipitate the beginning of the end of the United kingdom? What a tragedy when all the Brexiteers really wanted was to get rid of all the "foreigners" that have overwhelmed this country. The ones that do all the jobs the indigenous population don't want to do, like picking the crops in the fields or keeping the health service running.

18/10/19

Oliver Letwin, has today put forward a motion the there will be no vote on Boris's big deal until the underpinning legislation is in place and understood. If passed this would this would effectively push the date for Boris's deal past the required for the initiation of the so called Benn act. Effectively this means that legally Boris Johnson must apply to the EU for an extended Brexit deadline. Why is Oliver Letwin doing this? Probably because Boris has always implied that he has a way to get round the Benn act as well as the lack of legal text attached to the deal at this time.

19/10/19

This is the first time in 38 years that parliament had a sitting on a Saturday on that occasion it was related to the Falklands war. The stated reason for this extraordinary sitting was to ratify the agreement that Boris Johnson has procured from the EU two days ago. Prime Minister Boris Johnson's plan was to obtain this ratification without providing any legal underpinning text. A little like signing a blank cheque! This situation was curtailed by Oliver Letwin's bill which was passed by 322 votes to 306. Following this defeat Boris decided that parliament was not "playing his game" so he decided to take home his metaphorical ball and not play again until Monday.

Boris has now sent a letter to the EU requesting an extension to the deadline thus meeting his legal obligations under the Benn act. Although it seems he has not signed this document, question is does this invalidate the legality of the said document? As well this letter Boris also sent another spelling out his perceived consequences of granting an extension, all negative as one might expect. This one, is signed, so what is the ploy. Is he trying to circumvent the rule of law, is this some form distraction tactics? Many pundits still suggest his primary agenda is a "no deal" Brexit.

Monday 20$^{th}$ sees a court case pertaining to the Benn act, to be heard in Scotland, the details at this point are a little scant. The material content will no doubt emerge tomorrow.

So many Brexiteers consider that acceptance of the so called deal, spoof or otherwise, will end the misery of the ongoing saga. How wrong can they be, this would merely mark "the end of the beginning". Deal or no deal, regardless of which new trade deals, would be needed to fill the vacuum of diminishing trade with the EU. Significant trade deals with EU , the USA or China would be critical to the future success story of the UK. These trade deals do not take place in weeks, months or even years in many cases. Those British people who do not like rules that are set by others, may have a bitter pill to swallow, in the form of significant compromise.

Some consideration should also be given to the peripheral trade arrangements associated with EU membership. Such as; the West Africa Agreement on Trade and Tariffs (WAATT). Canada, Japan, Norway and other potentially less significant countries.

The Extinction Rebellion has now finished its fortnight long demonstration in London. It is very clear that there exists a very strong lobby for environmental issues. The World stage has been open to Greta Thunberg the 16 year Swedish girl accusing world leaders and politicians of denying her and her global peers the right to a long and healthy life. This issue perhaps should be at the top of everyone's agenda! There aren't any trade deals on a dead planet. Zero carbon and carbon neutral are becoming the mantra of many progressive businesses and as environmental issues take on an ethical dimension the marketeers will latch on to the potential to, both differentiate their products and provide competitive advantage. The EU and indeed the UK has been a the forefront of carbon reduction, the problem is how does this square with the new trade deals a Brexit Britain will be seeking with countries like the USA and China, the two most polluting countries on the planet by far. Does Brexit Britain buy steel from the USA, produced in its furnaces fired by coal from it's newly opened mines, as part of Trump's make America great again campaign. President Trump of course withdrew from the Paris accord on climate change, dismissing it as false news and scaremongering.

## 20/10/19

Today John Bercow, ruled against the same motion as Saturday being put forward again, sighting that there was no significant change in the last two days. John Bercow was criticised for being biased by several Tory MPs. The court case in Scotland relating to the Benn act was suspended pending additional evidence, So a little bit of a nothing day apart from a blame game. Tomorrow may see the first reading of the withdrawal bill. Potential amendments could be; acceptance conditional on a further peoples vote i.e. referendum. Which could be Boris's deal or remain, extending the customs union to the whole of the UK, or other. Let's hope that Jeremy Corbyn is a little more effective, than today, he was about as much use as a "chocolate fire guard, " although he does look a little poorly. Perhaps this would be a good time to stand down and let kier Starmer take over the leadership of the Labour party. This would likely infer a wider credibility to the electorate.

## 22/10/19

Well it's turbulent Tuesday, a promising day on the horizon, but who knows? Plenty of adverse comments on social media relating to John Bercow's ruling yesterday in parliament. As per usual vindictive and venomous as opposed to well considered and constructive, surely the British people are better than this. Our members of parliament have been democratically elected to represent our best interests, surely the least the British people can do is to listen carefully to what is being said, prior to making reasoned and well argued comments. Currently the core British principles of fairness, understanding and tolerance are sadly not evident. Today could see the likely direction Boris's deal will go.

Vote on the so called divorce bill $2^{nd}$ reading for 329 against 299, a Boris win. The next vote is about the time table for completion Boris was expecting to complete in two or three days in order to put this back to the EU for ratification and completion on the $31^{st}$ October. This vote for 308 against 322 Boris loses, making it virtually impossible to compete by $31^{st}$ October.

23/10/19

Many are thinking why did parliament vote for Boris's deal, when it was clearly inferior to Theresa May's offering? Maybe Boris Johnson had set a trap for parliament, had they voted his deal down the only option left was no deal. Quite clearly the EU has no appetite whatsoever for reopening further negotiations. Parliament by voting for the deal in principle, now have the opportunity to scrutinise and amend the implementation of the deal. For example making its implementation conditional on a public vote. As no deal is not an option then a people's vote "referendum" would be a straight forward choice Boris's "fantastic deal" or remain in the EU. "Simples" even Sergei the meerkat understands that. As Kenneth Clarke suggested in points of order yesterday evening after Boris put the proceedings on pause. "Surely the solution to this is to gain a short extension from the EU and get this thing done". Brexit has been 3 years plus in the making what difference are a few more days going to make, a small compromise from Boris surely. Or indeed is he concerned that closer scrutiny might expose further weaknesses within his deal. From a positive perspective closer scrutiny may develop amendments that could make Boris's deal more palatable to a broader electorate. Thus contributing to the rebuilding of the unity that has been lost in the UK over recent years.

Brexiteers demand the return of sovereignty to the British Parliament, that has been taken away by these nasty Europeans, it would seem they really want sovereignty only when it supports their agendas. It would seem quite strange that that those most mistrusting of the EU, would want to sign a cheque for 39 billion pounds without first checking the terms and conditions of the deal, it's a little like buying a house from the pictures in the estate agents window.

24/10/19

Boris's response to this situation; it's Jeremy Corbyn's fault stymieing everything, Ian Blackwell whinged about Scotland voting to remain in the EU and not being consulted, Jo Swinson and the liberal Democrats for being undemocratic, and of course those nasty Europeans that are putting the interests of 508 million EU citizens ahead of our 62 million. How dare they.

So his decision let's have a general election on December 12th, which would in essence be a quasi referendum. More smoke and mirrors, what has happened with "let's get it done". Perhaps he is beginning to regret voting against Theresa May's deal when she was prime minister. Of course misogyny does not exist in the conservative party, they have had two female prime ministers to labour's none.

So what are the options at this point?

The best deal on the table is the one we already have, this could be achieved simply be revoking article 50. As a consequence of this the 37% of the electorate that voted Brexit in the referendum, could become very disillusioned and disenfranchised to the point of civil disobedience. Recent research shows many people are demonstrating extremely polarised perspectives to the point of total intransigence to or denial of any other views. Unfortunately, it can also be said that a high majority fall back onto racist arguments to substantiate their points of view. This is not an option without considerable risk.

The precise opposite is to leave without a deal, an absolute clean break Brexit. World Trade Organisation (WTO) Tariffs would apply immediately, which would increase the average cost of all goods by 10% imported from the EU and other countries that are part of EU trade agreements, such as Japan, Canada, Norway, West Africa trade group and others not quite so significant. The UK could reciprocate by invoking pro rata WTO charges. However administration cost would be very high, and this would run against the mantra of hard line

Brexiteers i.e. A free trade UK. Inevitability leading to a border in Ireland which potentially could cast the Good Friday agreement to the wind. Polarising Republican and Unionist positions once again setting the peace process back years. Scottish Nationalists would be invigorated towards independence and under these circumstances may well be successful, United kingdom no more!!

Boris's deal, is not good for the unionist element in Northern Ireland by threatening the integrity of the UK. From this perspective this deal is not as watertight as Theresa May's deal. And once again the Scottish Nationalists would use the continued EU customs union as a lever towards achieving their own agenda.

Boris's deal put to a referendum against revoke article 50, or Boris's deal with a wider application of the EU customs union. Which ever referendum would seem to be a good compromise, because at this point it would seem compromise is the only way forward.

A general election might change the numbers, but can it solve the problems or indeed any the options or combinations of the above?

27/10/19

Jo Swinson and Ian Blackwell are preparing to propose a December 9th election. The EU look set to offer a 3 month extension but no renegotiation of the so called divorce agreement. How Jeremy Corbyn will "run with this" remains to be seen.

28/10/19

Parliament today a little like a children's party where they just about stopped short of throwing the cakes at each other. Boris unsurprisingly lost the vote for a general election on 12th December. The EU have granted a three month flextention, so Brexit could take place 30th November, 31st December or 31st January 2020.

29/10/19

Boris Johnson seems a little gung ho about the prospects of an election, he may have good reason to be so. Jeremy Corbyn it would seem is still slipping in the polls, with his all things to all people approach. Mr Corbyn says he wants a general election, but questionably are his tactics really aimed at preventing a no deal Brexit or is he taking the opportunity to "kick the can a little further down the road."

30/10/19

Well it's a 12<sup>th</sup> December election, so despite the children's party of 2 days ago Parliament have decided the 3 days difference in dates is not really worth arguing about. Will this election solve the conundrum? The amount of potential outcomes are mind blowing. Boris Johnson once again throwing smoke and mirrors along with a cornucopia of confusion into the arena. Surely a simple referendum based on Boris's deal or remain would have been much better and clear cut. Or is it that Boris can't rely on the British people to make the same mistake twice.

No votes for 16 year olds or settled EU nationals, wonder why that could be, perhaps the same reason why Boris and friends don't like the second referendum as a solution to the conundrum. Clearly there exists a greater potential for a referendum to resolve this impasse than a general election. A straight vote based on Boris's "amazing" deal versus remain. The general election approach could potentially leave a much worse situation than currently exists, hung parliament or indeed if Boris Johnson wins, no deal will be back on the table. Boris's deal was only ever a token deal that could have been the catalyst leading to the demise of the United kingdom.

31/10/19

Today is the day, "do or die" is dead in the water. Jo Swinson makes her first error of the election campaign! Challenging Boris Johnson to a live three way debate that didn't include the SNP, with whom she had been working to help bring about the forthcoming election, whoops. Jeremy Corbyn made an excellent opening speech for the Labour party election campaign, he said most things must people want to hear; more NHS, more police officers, protection of jobs and workers rights. Investment in infrastructure a new deal from the EU that will form one option in a people's vote. Ie a referendum between Jeremy's deal or remain. So this at least does provide a mechanism for closure of the Brexit issue.

01/11/19

Donald Trump opens the batting today managing two broadsides in one go, not that he would dream of interfering in British politics! He said that Jeremy Corbyn was bad news and could take the UK into bad places. Of Boris Johnson he outlined what a good guy he was, but his deal with the EU was "none to good" and certainly didn't provide a good background for a trade deal with the USA. He also pointed out what a good guy Nigel Farage is and how him and Boris should work together, as if that is likely!! Well not in public anyway.

In fairness Boris and his ERG compatriots, have a lot in common with Nigel Farage, both have a no deal Brexit as a default option. Boris could have done without his fellow New Yorker (D,Trump) pointing out what a "bum deal" he had negotiated with the EU. He knew that already, but unfortunately for Boris the electorate now also know it was a Theresa May deal, with the words backstop removed and the Irish border moved to the middle of the Irish sea.

Nigel Farage has emerged this morning, informing Boris Johnson, that his Brexit party are ready and will be placing 500 candidates into the forthcoming general election. He states that he is aware that this could split the Brexit vote, subsequently letting Jeremy Corbyn in via the back door. As such he is proposing what he terms a "leave alliance". This means not challenging each other in selected seats where remainers could win if the vote was split between Brexit and Conservative parties. This needs to happen fairly quickly, ie before the candidates are registered.

Whilst considering Nigel Farage and those that can't resist conspiracy theories. Recent theories have emerged suggesting that Nigel Farage is on a pro USA payroll who's aim is to "make America great again" and that Farage's brief is to destroy the European Union, this because the EU is seen an even bigger threat to American supremacy than China, frequently collectively topping the GDP of the USA. Should the UKs contribution to the GDP of the EU be removed then this would significantly increase USAs power in the trading stakes game. But of course this doesn't happen in the real world!

02/11/19

Yesterday evening Laura Kuenssberg, the BBC's political editor, asked Boris about President Trump's comments relating to his EU exit deal i.e. it was a bad deal, and if implemented would represent a significant obstacle towards a trade deal with USA. Boris applied his usual approach when he doesn't have a scripted answer, lots of waffle with little realistic content, but by implication suggesting Trump's words were meaningless rhetoric that has probably been taken out of context. Laura Kuenssberg went on to ask, "would you say the same about Mr Trump's NHS comments" that it would not form part of a trade deal. This part of Trump's rhetoric met with Boris's total approval. A little surprising he hadn't anticipated those questions, and not having a Dominic Cummings penned script at hand, with a really clever answer.

Today Boris has rejected Nigel Farage's offer of a "leave alliance". So will Nigel Farage put up 500 candidates next week, or was it a bluff to put Boris back on the no deal track?

03/11/19

Some interesting news emerging from ASEAN (Association of South East Asian Nations) and its FTA (Free Trade Association) partners his weekend. This Monday there will be a meeting to discuss a possible free trade agreement between the two organisations, a so called Regional Comprehensive Economic Partnership (RCEP) which would include countries such as China, India, South Korea, Australia, New Zealand, Singapore and many others, 16 in all. The potential of this partnership could turn world economics on its head, watch this space Mr Trump and indeed Mr Johnson and his little

Englander Brexit brigade. Mr Trump will tell him the rules of nature; big is powerful, small is weak.

The deadline date for registration of candidates for the forthcoming general election is November 15$^{th}$. Nigel Farage says he will not be standing himself, but will be supporting the 600 Brexit party candidates, that's 100 more than yesterday, perhaps he is just raising the stakes.

04/11/19

New speaker today Sir Lyndsey Hoyle, best of luck!!

Nigel Farage opened the Brexit party election campaign today, very eloquent, with superb presentation skills. The content was largely conjecture, some emphasis on Boris's lack of cooperation with his plan for tactical voting, or giving up the "Boris plan". The main problem with Nigel Farage and the Brexit party it would seem is lack content in terms measurable factors such as what benefits will Brexit deliver; more jobs, better pay, new laws, what are the plans for current and emerging industries, how would freedom of movement throughout the world be affected? How can the Good Friday agreement be honoured? How could Scottish independence be dealt with? What trade proposals and principles would be put to the USA? Will trade deals lost as a result of leaving the EU be rekindled such as Japan, Canada, West Africa agreement etc? Will we have our own environmental rules, will they lag or lead the rest of the world?

05/11/19

Philip Hammond (ex chancellor of the exchequer) announces his retirement from politics. Many would say he jumped before he was pushed, not having his whip reinstated, as some other conservatives did after citing their concerns about a no deal Brexit. What some people are putting on social media, is nothing short of heart-breaking, suggesting he is a traitor, should be the one who is dead in ditch, how some would like to wipe that stupid grin off his face and it goes on and on, hardly anything pleasant or complimentary. This man who was chancellor of the exchequer, had all the facts and figures, had the audacity to warn his peers of the substantive risks of no deal Brexit. To add insult to injury when questioned relating to the risks associated with a no deal Brexit by one of the political pundits. Philip Hammond had the temerity to tell the truth. What ever next a conservative government member telling the truth, anyone would think the future of the country was at stake.

Jeremy Corbyn opened the labour party election campaign today, with clear concise and well defined objectives, his presentation compelling and acceptably detailed for an opening gambit. Considerable focus on the NHS with a well reasoned explanation of the likelihood of this becoming part of trade negotiations with the USA. Jeremy also explained how the Labour party intended to bring about unity not only between leavers and remainers, but the UK as a whole. This in terms of the context of and the potential consequences of Boris's deal. He explained labour's timetable for negotiations with the EU and the proposed referendum. This would be represented by two choices; Jeremy Corbyn's deal or remain. Some would say including Nigel Farage this is "a vote to remain or remain" in the EU.

Jo Swinson opened the liberal Democrats election campaign today.

Nigel Farage had a bit of a setback, it would seem that giving up the "Boris plan" was a risk too far, for twenty Brexit party candidates, quitting before they started.

Boris says no to Brexit party alliance

Savid Javid knows every intimate detail of Labour's spending plans, but doesn't seem to know too much about the Conservatives own plans.

This week is the 30th anniversary of the bringing down of the Berlin wall and 70 years since the end of the Berlin airlift. As well being Remembrance week, this is week where we choose to forget all the things we need to remember, as to why we had two world wars. Yes we remember the dead, but not the reason they gave their lives.

On page 33 the following comment was added;

> *"How can anyone watching the 75th D day anniversary commemorations in 2019 fail to believe in unity within Europe?*
>
> *It was a unity of that won this war, now let this unity win the peace".* (draft copy)

One of the Brexit supporting draft copy readers of this publication made the following comments relating to the above statement;

> *"The astonishing ignorance of the statement that European unity won the war. No mention of Britain standing alone until with the help of Commonwealth forces and then USA liberated*

*the European continent from another European force. The formation of NATO funded in large part by USA and Britain has been the primary reason for subsequent peace."*

Clearly a lapse of memory, it was of course the USA with; John Wayne, Robert Mitcham, and Henry Fonda who won the war. This with a little help from the Brits in the form of Richard Burton and Richard Todd, (The Longest Day 1962).

Sorry John, couldn't resist it.


Protagonists of the European project have long had concerns relating to the structure and management of NATO. Whilst the unity it brings within Europe has certainly been a cornerstone paving the way towards the peace now enjoyed across the European continent with notable exceptions of course. The problem for Europe is that the USA is the single largest contributor to NATO, both in financial terms and shear military clout. Whilst NATO financing is based on 2% of GDP, collectively the EU could potentially equal that of the USA contribution, assuming all members "paid up" in full, a bone of contention for President Trump, but that's another story. So in general terms "he who plays the fiddle calls the tune". In the main

NATO has worked well since its inception in 1949, presiding over the reunification of Germany, the Bosnian crisis and the invasion of Kuwait by Saddam Hussein, all to an apparently satisfactory conclusion. Some would say NATO or the power of NATO brought about the unravelling of the Soviet Union another potential "European dictatorship". The real worry for Europeans are the gung-ho Republicans like George Bush jnr who took NATO and Europe, totally unnecessarily into a second gulf war with Saddam Hussein's Iraq. Or Donald Trump who has the world's "biggest button".

Those of a more cynical disposition frequently question the United States real agenda, for example WW2 started September 1939 when Germany one of the so called Axis powers invaded Poland. The Axis powers being Germany, Italy and Japan. Some historian suggest WW2 started in 1937 when Japan invaded China. However in response to the invasion of Poland, 2 days later France and the United Kingdom declared war on Germany. In the2 years that followed, Germany and its allies Italy and to some extent Spain, conquered or annexed most of Europe. Still no direct involvement from the USA, other than selling arms to the UK, which amassed to £21 billion for the duration of the war. In 1939 UK GDP was around £3 billion, by 1945 this had grown to £10 billion, hence an average of around £6.5 billion for the duration of the war. Meaning that the accrued war loan equated more than 3 times the UKs annual GDP. In present day terms this is representative of circa £8 trillion i.e. 3 times £2.7 trillion The UKs current GDP, now that's some loan! That doesn't account for interest either. Perhaps Winston Churchill's famous speech of February 1941 should be rewritten, he famously said *"Give us the tools and we will finish the job"* or more appropriately *"Sell us the tools and we will finish the job"* this nearly a year before the Americans decided to join the Allies. When on December 7th 1941 the Japanese launched a surprise attack on Pearl Harbour, sinking and damaging many battleships, as well as killing and wounding around 3500 US personnel. Enter the USA into WW2.

Clearly the Americans involvement shifted the balance of power and facilitated the winning of the war, perhaps just in time. Nazi Germany in 1944 was literally months away from the development of an atomic bomb, as were of course the Americans and the British. The war with Germany ended with an unconditional surrender May 8th 1945.

Three months later two American atomic bombs brought down the final curtain on WW2. The first on

Hiroshima 6th August 1945 and the second on Nagasaki 9th August 1945 Thank God both sides didn't have these weapons, the potential for Armageddon wasn't so far away.

My contributor's assertion that The USA and UK won WW2, is it would seem quite a common perspective, possibly perpetrated by the Hollywood movie moguls, as previously mentioned. This perspective tends to imply a passive role for the majority of European countries as suggested earlier. The Soviet Union for example joined the Allies six months before the USA, losing 25 million of its citizens as a direct result of standing up to the WW2 Nazis, and yes it is 25 million, not a misprint, and representative of 14.2% of its population,

Poland lost  6.0 million people 17.2% of population.
Yugoslavia  1.7 million people, 11% of population.
Greece      416,000 people 6.6% of population.
France      810,000 people 1.9% of population.
Et al.

This does not look much like "passive intervention" particularly when compared to those of:

UK.    386,000 people, 0.8% of population.
USA    405,000 people, 0.3 of population

When measured in terms of Human life, heartache and broken families, who paid the highest cost?

As insignificant as it may seem at this point, on 31st December 2006 the UK fully repaid the outstanding balance of USA war loan to the tune of £45 million, having taken 60 years to repay.

NATO no doubt on balance has been a force for good in Europe, but arguably only when it benefits the USA. Those who dismiss the validity of this statement might like to answer the following questions.

What was the agenda of the USA with respect to Bosnia and the Balkans?

What actions did the USA take when the UK and France both key members of NATO invaded Egypt in the so called Suez crisis?

What actions did NATO take when Argentina invaded the Falkland Islands?

Why the second Gulf War, what was it really about?

11/11/19

Nigel Farage says Brexit candidates won't stand against Conservatives that won their seats in the last election, not a pact of course. Even though, Donald Trump said,"I told them they need to work together." Is this the beginning of a no deal stitch up of the British people?

Overall all parties are making so many promises, that it could make sense to have a general every year. That way after about ten years, and all the promises fulfilled, we could all be living in Utopia.

12/11/19

One  week into electioneering and Boris scores another own goal by Boris needing Jeremy Corbyn to tell him the unprecedented flooding in Yorkshire, Lincolnshire Nottinghamshire and Derbyshire is a national emergency.

13/11/19

Boris rolls up in the flood areas, and didn't get a good reception. Jeremy Corbyn goes to Scotland for a bad reception, relating to a second referendum on Scottish independence. Jo Swinson has her battle bus blocked in by anti austerity campaigners, based on the past Liberal Democrat coalition with the conservatives.

Farage starts talking tactics again, withdrawing candidates from selected seats to enhance a Brexit supporting outcome. Wonder what has gone on behind the scenes? Is a no deal Brexit back on the hidden agenda again, perhaps it has never been off it.

14/11/19

Figures out today; NHS waiting times worst since 2001, so much focus back on the NHS. Jeremy Corbyn gaining some political capital out of the situation, reiterating his large scale commitment.

Still no manifestos as yet!

Worryingly recent small scale research suggests that many voters, seem to be of the opinion that Boris Johnson will win the election with a majority, such that he can "get Brexit done" with his self labelled "fantastic deal" that he says bares "no resemblance to the Theresa May deal"or so Boris says, the one that he voted against, 3 times (see comments 17/10/19). So in general terms most of the Brexiteers and quite a few naïve remainers of the electorate are expecting that Brexit will happen on the 31<sup>st</sup> January 2020, and that will be it, job done, no more Brexit. Now who's living in "cloud cuckoo land."

Although leaving the EU on the 31<sup>st</sup> is quite feasible, Brexit being over is just wishful thinking. The next phase is the difficult part, with the 12 month remaining transition period, coupled to the expectations of delivering a comprehensive trade deal with the EU at the end of it. Boris has already stated "there will be no extension to this date" This by definition leaves the gate wide open for a no deal exit from the EU. Just what the ERG and Nigel Farage wanted and just what Boris Johnson has been working toward. So we can all look forward to some more "kicking the can down the road punctuated no doubt by meaningless so called negotiations aimed at keeping the no deal protagonists at bay until it's too late. Whoops a no deal Brexit.

15/11/19

Jeremy Corbyn seems to be having a momentary lapse of reason today, suggesting everyone has high speed broadband for free, and who is going to pay for it? Google, Amazon, Microsoft and the like, by paying more taxes, sounds good. These multi nationals will agree without a mummer, or perhaps they may offset this by making charges for things they currently offer for free, like Gmail accounts, basic access to YouTube, Spotify etc.

Boris is picking a squabble with the EU relating to the selection of a commissioner.. Subject to universal acceptance of Boris's deal, the UK will remain in the EU until 31$^{st}$ December 2020 as part of the transition agreement. This means the UK still has an obligation to nominate a commissioner to cover that timeframe. Boris is refusing to do so, probably just a friendly gesture to the EU in order to lubricate the wheels of negotiations of the exit trade deal!!

16/11/19

Some suggestion today that the conservatives are attempting to bribe Brexit candidates to stand down, Anne Widdecombe in particular although a little sketchy on detail at the moment.

17/11/2019

Jennifer Arcuri a business person who benefited from a business deal orchestrated by Boris Johnson when he was London mayor, now seems to be dishing the dirt on him, via the, you've guessed it, the Daily Mail. All the usual he said, she said and associated innuendo.

19/11/2019

Party leaders are today presenting themselves to the Confederation of British Industry (CBI), as the risk of a no deal Brexit seems not to be abating in any shape or form at the moment. However if we listen to the likes of Nigel Farage, Jacob Rees-Mogg and his ERG cronies as well Boris Johnson they will consistently repeat the mantra "no deal is better than a bad deal" that being said the Johnson deal is certainly not good deal for the Scottish people or the Irish. The terrible trio will miss no opportunity to extol the virtues and opportunities afforded by a clean break Brexit. Sad thing is they are plentiful in conjecture, but short on the detail of how, what, when and who. The likelihood is that delivery of these wonderful opportunities will fall on the many members of the CBI (Confederation of British Industry) that really believe that leaving the EU is detrimental to the British economy. The Daily Mail today describes CBI members as fat cats living in ivory towers, as if to alienate them from the process of making Brexit work. At the end of the day without the entrepreneurs and investors associated with the

CBI it certainly won't work. The politicians that are providing the so called opportunities of Brexit as well having an ability to negotiate global scale deals in months rather than years. When you consider that Boris in 84 days managed to get "a fantastic deal" with the EU. A deal that basically removed the word backstop from the narrative of Theresa May's deal and moved the northern Ireland border to the Irish sea to provide a game changing deal that even Boris couldn't even explain in a coherent format. Will these politicians make Brexit or will the hard-line Brexiteers that are convinced that we can rewrite the rule book and do trade on our terms, the people that can tell you all the problems, but never have any tangible solutions, other than pull up the drawbridges and keep Johnny foreigner out.

The fact remains the entrepreneurs, investors, and business people are the people carrying the burden of success, whatever the outcome. So why don't we listen to what they have to say. Most will suggest the best deal is the one we already have, within the EU. There are dissenters amongst their ranks of course such as Tim Martin (Wetherspoons) or James Dyson, of course very successful, business people, but needless to say with their own agendas. Which by looking at their business activities, one can make their own judgment?

20/11/2019

If you read the Guardian then Jeremy Corbyn won the debate conversely if you read the Daily Mail then Boris won. In general terms it would seem to be about even stevens. Jeremy Corbyn took some flack relating to anti-Semitism. This would seem to be more semantics than substance. It would seem on the face of it, that charge of anti-Semitism against Jeremy Corbyn relates to his sympathetic approach to the plight of the Palestinian people, who it would seem are having their homeland systematically stolen from them by the Israeli people and their forces. Up until a few days ago the United States government supported the assertion that Israeli settlements on the occupied west bank were in breach of international law. The Trump administration has now reversed this position held by the US state department since 1978.

21/11/2019

The manifestos are now emerging, Labour key points from the perspective of this narrative; new Brexit deal to be negotiated with the EU and put to a referendum on the form of Jeremy Corbyn's deal or remain. Large spending on infrastructure including nationalisation of many public services such as railways, broadband communications, royal mail, water and power.

Liberal Democrats to revoke article 50, with no new referendum. Nigel Farage wants to ditch Boris's deal and leave the EU without a deal. The conservatives will no doubt promote Boris's deal or no deal with no extensions beyond the December 2020 deadline.

Jo Swinson may have made an error of judgement with her revoke article 50 stance, this potentially will alienate 37% of the electorate that voted Brexit, if she thinks they were convinced by misleading rhetoric like Boris Johnson's NHS bus statement and the kippers that were subjected to EU bureaucracy and subsequently turned out to be UK government bureaucracy. Then Jo Swinson should, or needs to substantiate her reasoning. Or when people say to her "you are defying the will of 17 plus million people in this country" perhaps she should respond with "I am trying to protect the future of the 66 plus million population of the UK". Let us not forget members of parliament are elected to represent the best interests of the whole nation not just those on the electoral register that have chosen to vote. Too many members of parliament say and do, what gets them re-elected, it much easier than persuading people there may be a better way.

A pact has now emerged in Wales between Plaid Cymru, the Green party and the Liberal Democrats. This is where, any of these parties in Wales has a chance of winning a specific seat, then the other 2 parties will stand down. Plaid Cymru suggesting the best way to reject Brexit in Wales is to vote for Plaid Cymru, but baring in mind that Wales in the referendum voted to leave. Has the potential damage to the Welsh farming become more evident, we await with baited breath.

25/11/2019

Viewing the main party's manifestos i.e. Conservative, Labour, Liberal Democrats, the DUP and the SNP. They all seem like a long list of all the things they should have done in the past, but somehow didn't manage it for reasons beyond their control. On the face of it, if a general election were to be held every year for the next ten years with all the politicians fulfilling all their promises like they suggest they can, then Utopia would be there for the taking!!

Just a few keys points from a cynical perspective; The Conservatives having reduced the national police force by twenty thousand officers in the recent past, have under their watch created a crime wave. Boris Johnson has committed to fix this crime wave, making "the streets of our great country safe again." What inspired and innovative solution does he have? He is going to recruit twenty thousand new police officers. This is the sort of intuitive thinking we need. Jeremy Corbyn's nationalisation plans have been dealt a blow by Scottish and Southern Energy, they have set up a holding company in Switzerland, thus potentially impeding nationalisation of this entity. Plus ringing alarm bells relating to the immense losses encountered by many shareholders in Railtrack especially those of the so called "hard working ordinary British people" who lost their hard earned cash, on what should have been a relatively safe investment.

Jo Swinson's hard line position of revoking article 50 without offering significant reasoning to pacify the 17 million plus voters expecting Brexit to happen. This has the potential to become Swinson's swansong.

The SNP are playing heavily on independence, probably being their strongest opportunity yet to achieve that end. The DUP are strongly backing the Brexit line even though Northern Ireland voted to remain in the EU. Particularly worrying when this has the effect of polarising politics in Northern Ireland once again, with Sinn Fein suggesting the only solution is a United Ireland. So all in all much as expected.

27/11/2019
The chief Rabbi of the UK says people should not vote labour because of the anti-Semitism in its ranks.
Boris also has a few problems on his favourite subject, Islamophobia with a Conservative candidate being withdrawn from Glasgow.

Michael Heseltine (Conservative) has thrown a brickbat into the Conservatives campaign, with a keynote speech for the Liberal Democrat party, somewhat a reality check for those Brexiteers not in denial.

28/11/2019

Michael Heseltine's speech perhaps not so keynote, the BBC cutting it off whilst live, and subsequently only showing the part where he describes the stop Brexit pledge of Jo Swinson, being a little naïve is this censorship? The Daily Mail not apparently even making mention of it, but as one would expect well covered by the Guardian, clearly with much less impact given the imbalance of the readership. His key points were related to the successes of the European project, the potential economic impact, the risks of putting "most of the eggs in the north American basket" and the likely delays to any deals, which could be many years in the making. A man of Michael Heseltine's experience and service having served under Churchill and many prime ministers of substance such as Margaret Thatcher, Harold Macmillan, etc. It could be reasonable to suppose that a statesman of his calibre deserves a much larger platform than he was given by the media.

29/11/2019

Today the Daily Mail seems to have Boris in their sights. This for articles he wrote 25 years ago, which are misogynistic, and derogatory to blue collar male working class people. Is this distraction tactics, levelling so much interest in a pathetic and ill-informed article of a quarter century ago. Whilst failing to comment constructively on a speech by an elder statesman two days ago relating to the potential disaster of Brexit. Is the daily mail engaging in gamesmanship? Trying to make it look like the opposition are engaging in a smear campaign.

30/11/19

No comments today, unfortunately electioneering has been suspended, as a result of a terrorist incident on London bridge again. Let us hope no one makes any political capital out of this, another unfortunate tragedy, for all of us.

01/12/19

Boris just can't resist it, the terror attack was Labour's fault and Ken Clarke didn't help according to Boris Johnson. Politicians should be setting high moral, social, ethical and compassionate standards as well as a strong propensity towards leadership. These qualities wouldn't seem very evident in either Boris Johnson or his close associates, Rees-Mogg, Duncan Smith, Javid, Cummings etc.

02/12/19

Well today really takes the biscuit, Jeremy Corbyn has blamed Donald Trump, for the latest London bridge terror attack. Just hours before Trumps state visit to the UK for a NATO summit. This is just about the same level as a street brawl. None of these men are fit to run a drinks party in a brewery. Two far right wing clowns and a leftist that sees himself as some kind of Fidel Castro. The whole situation takes respect and responsibility down to gutter level. No wonder "the hard working British people" are confused and totally under whelmed.

03/12/19

Just a few days ago Jeremy Corbyn came by some documentation that clearly shows the government are and have been in negotiations with the USA relating to health provision in the UK, with which he challenged the Government. Basically the response was that the documents had been taken out of context, begging the question misunderstanding or lie? Today in the Daily Telegraph there is a suggestion that the said documents may be Russian interference in the form of "false news" or fabrication. At this point the Government is still refusing to release the intelligence and security committee report relating to Russian interference in the EU referendum of 2016. Could this affect the potential outcome of the general election. Should this be the case, is it morally right to continue to withhold this report?

04/12/20

President Trump seemed to blow Jeremy Corbyn's boats out of the water yesterday, telling the world he "wouldn't want the NHS even if it were handed to him on a silver platter" On the face of it a sweeping statement of definitive meaning. Just consider how much so called NHS work is contracted out to private hospitals, a vast proportion of ophthalmic and dental work is contracted to private suppliers, so it is not really difficult to contemplate how many NHS activities could potentially be taken by attrition. Pharmaceuticals are big business, billions of pounds are spent by the NHS on American pharmaceutical products each year, many at better prices than those available to customers in the USA. It is probably a little naive to contemplate this as insignificant or no go area. So Jeremy Corbyn is reasonably asking why has something that is non-negotiable, been a subject of negotiations?

NATO was high on the agenda today, President Trump, wouldn't seem to be Mr popular having differences of opinion with Emanuel Macron, and Justin Trudeau, but nothing to influence Brexit.

05/12/19

More promises from Boris today, £100 tax cut almost immediately, new laws on health tourism and rail strikes. Most people would rather have pot hole free roads to drive on, that would save more money for the hard working British people in the long run. Heath tourism legislation should help to completely eliminate the EHIC (European Health Insurance Card), and put costs up for medical procedures carried out within the EU. Strike laws relating to rail travel, does this signpost the beginning of dismantling all the employment laws introduced as a result of being in the EU. Should Boris prevail in this election the mantra "hard working British people" will soon be replaced by "if you want more money you will have to work harder."

07/12/19

The last debate between the two prospective prime ministers, not very inspiring, same old, same old, might as well have been tweedledum and tweedledee . If these are the best potential leaders available then heaven help us. Today on BBC TV news some mention again relating to the source of Jeremy Corbyn's "leaked NHS documents" and again suggesting some involvement of the Russians. In the absence of confirmation or denial from the Conservatives, it can only be deduced that the meetings did take place, but that the content may or may not be a representative transcript.

Much talk in the general media about tactical voting, with perhaps Labour preferring their disenchanted voters to vote Brexit party in the hope that this action will dilute the Conservative vote as well as many other potential combinations. Which in essence serve to highlight the inadequacies of the voting system. Generally speaking the more candidates the worse the situation becomes. This unfortunately will continue to be the case, we have already had a referendum on proportional representation. This was rejected mainly because the implications and potential benefits weren't clearly understood by the electorate, with the waters being muddied by the mainstream parties, probably because they had the most to lose. Had proportional representation been accepted, not only would the elected parliament be more representative of "the will of the people," but the structure would be less partisan and more democratic, thus potentially delivering a route towards parliamentary sovereignty as opposed to partisan autocracy.

08/11/19

More pressure on Jeremy Corbyn today relating to Anti-Semitism yet again! As some apparently new documentation has emerged. Will this go away, or will this be tomorrow's next revelation?

09/12/19

Looks like Anti-Semitism had a rest-day today. The Daily Mirror carried a front page story of a 4 year old being treated for pneumonia on the floor of Leeds Royal infirmary, Boris seemed to try to play it down, so really just more tit for tat. With Labour jumping on the bandwagon. No doubt the Conservatives will counter this tomorrow with yet another revelation. If this wasn't so serious it could be really entertaining. People interviewed in the media, and directly seem to just want it all to end. Sadly this, it is suggested is a very disillusioned perspective. Two days to go Friday 13th looms closer. Will it be the billionaire brigade who see working people as cannon fodder and England as the Singapore of the North. Or will it be those that consider the best solution to every problem is throwing as much money as possible at it, until the problem goes away, allied to a policy of nationalising everything that isn't bolted down.

Will we end up with a hung parliament? What are the possibilities? Perhaps a government of national unity, but who would lead this coalition? Cometh the hour cometh the man/woman. Certainly not Johnson or Corbyn, perhaps someone who has earned respect for honesty, transparency, empathy, understanding, whilst possessing a genuine caring nature, is what is needed. From labour maybe; Hillary Benn, Kier Starmer, Yvette Cooper or indeed for those with Conservative leanings Anna Soubry, Rory Stewart or even Theresa May, who did a much better job than she was given credit for. Boris and his back stabbing ERG chums certainly orchestrated her demise. Her deal was much better than Boris's cut and paste job, the DUP have since discovered that, hence they now don't support "Boris's fantastic deal". Most people seem to forget, we could have left the EU on 30th March 2019. This on a deal that was accepted by the DUP, but Boris and the so called ERG consistently voted against it. Of course the agenda was different then, Boris had his eye on Theresa May's job, and the ERG were hell bent on a clean break Brexit. But of course the

Conservatives are blaming Labour and Parliament for causing all the delays.

10/12/19

Ball back in labour's court today, a recorded telephone message between Labour frontbencher Jonathan Ashworth and Tory friend. With Jonathan Ashworth suggesting that Jeremy Corbyn was a threat to national security. Disclaiming this later as just a bit of banter. Doesn't this get a tad pathetic?

11/12/19

Last day of campaigning, can Labour serve up an ace? Hidden in the small print today, Mr Trump rears his head once again.

> *"The World Trade Organization is facing a major crisis as its appellate body loses its ability to rule on new dispute cases. The US has been blocking the appointment of new judges to protest against the way the WTO does business." (DW news)*

President Trump does not want rulings by external bodies taking precedence over USA laws. Does he have an agenda, is this part of a plan for the USA to dominate and control world trade? Making America great again as per Trump's electioneering mantra.

The destruction of the EU and the WTO would herald a clear run home. Is this conspiracy theory, conjecture, false news, scare mongering or a potential reality?

12/12/19

Well this is it, so is it going to be a contest where those with the most convincing lies win, or will a nation in denial see the reality of truth through the myriad of smoke and mirrors, created by many of our illustrious politicians.

First impressions suggest a very high poll with many local polling stations reporting queues and long waiting times, perhaps a good sign for democracy.

**Friday 13th December**

Well there may be an omen in this date, Boris Johnson has won a clear majority. A very happy Christmas to all, this may be the last for a very long time. So what happens next? Likelihood is that Boris and his chums from the ERG will rescind the legislation relating to a no deal Brexit. This of course is to strengthen their hand in negotiations of a trade deal with the European Union. They will also reinforce the deadline for these negotiations completing December 2020. The date set will not be extended, this with typical dead in a ditch certainty.

So from a reasoned perspective, the odds are on a final exit from the EU December 2020 without a deal, exactly as planned by Boris and Chums and of course our old friend Nigel Farage. Never in the course of human conflict have so many been conned by so few.

What changes are likely to happen as a result of this potential outcome; Nissan, Toyota and Honda, move their operations to Europe, surely this is not possible! Mr Johnson said this was just scaremongering by those wishing to undermine Brexit and of course Boris wouldn't lie would he! We will still have Vauxhall motors, but aren't they owned by Peugeot Citroen group, wonder what they will do? Well there's no future in the motor industry anyway, all these new electric cars are a bit of a myth, but we do have the ability to make batteries for them, they could be a good export. Will Airbus continue to produce wings for A380s etc. in Wales? Remembering the UK relinquished all its shareholding in Airbus, which currently aspires to the top slot world's leading aircraft manufacturer, particularly with the demise of Boeing, resultant of the unfortunate air accidents with the 737- 800 max.

Boris has never supported the expansion of Heathrow into a very significant international hub airport. If he is a man his word then this won't happen either, now Boris is in the driving seat.

HS2 will probably still go ahead, even if the price tag exceeds £100 billion, with technology that is likely to achieve obsolescence before completion of the project. All this for a not too considerable improvement in performance!

The SNP have faired well in the election, Scottish independence will now be back on the agenda after all the Scottish people did not want to leave the European Union by a far bigger margin than the leave lobby in the UK referendum. Coupled to a likely push from the Irish Republican movement towards a United Ireland. Particularly when the Irish sea border proves to be unworkable. Primarily by giving rise to massive developments in both black and grey markets, i.e. large scale smuggling and tariff evasion.

Does Boris Johnson really care about the UK his consultations never go much beyond the peripheries of the M25 or stockbroker belt. Although he has recently discovered the North, or cynically perhaps a lot of Brexiteers in Labour's heartland.

What will happen to the many ex-Patriots living in the EU and have not qualified or even applied for citizenship in their host countries. Will they be subjected by the EU to a Boris's Australian style immigration tests? Or is this going to be another "fine mess" Boris's whizz kids "have gotten us into".

With the stats now available for election it would seem that Boris and friends, the Conservatives, attracted 43.6% of the popular vote (364) seats, with labour at 32.2% (203) seats, Liberal Democrats 11.5%. (11) seats. From this it can be seen that a combination of Labour and Liberal Democrat votes are approximately equal to those of the Conservatives, but only achieving a total of 214 seats. When also considering the turnout was 67.3% then it can be said that only 29.3% of the total electorate voted for this new Conservative Government potentially for the next 5 years, with a majority of 80 seats over the cumulative total seats of ALL the other parties. This of course begs the question is this really a democracy, where these figures stand it looks more like an autocracy than a democracy, or at worst a dictatorship. As for Jo Swinson she paid the price for her honesty and lack of experience, alas it was Swinson's swan song, making no gains for the Lib-Dems and losing her parliamentary seat.

16/12/19

Pundits are suggesting that with, Boris Johnson's significant majority i.e. 80, he has the freedom to ignore the very nationalistic right wing elements in the Conservative party such as the ERG and go for a softer more pragmatic and reasoned approach to Brexit, that could bring about a refreshing unity to the United kingdom; Giving the Scots less concern over leaving the EU, The Irish more reason to work together and less reason and justification for a United Ireland.

International business, the stock market and economists seemed to relish the thought. As a result the stock market surged, sterling increased significantly against both the US dollar and the Euro. As well as a resultant sense of certainty and direction seemed to be evident. Whilst reassuring those remainers fearing a cliff edge disaster. Blue sky at last, perhaps Boris is the new messiah after all.

17/12/19

Well this euphoria didn't last long, Boris has now announced, he is going to put legislation in place to ensure that the final leaving date of December 2020, is enshrined in law following the transition period. This effectively puts a no deal Brexit firmly back on the table, as discussed at the beginning of this chapter. Guess what happened today; stock market down, sterling down, despair and uncertainty up. Boris Johnson, Nigel Farage, Steve Baker and the ERG cronies do not want a deal, so watch this space! When taking into account the thinking of conspiracy theorists, then neither do Donald Trump, Vladimir Putin or Xi Jinping who's key aims are "to divide and conquer," i.e. to disempower the European Union.

The well known saying "they think it's all over, it is now" doesn't apply in its entirety, a vast majority of the electorate, are under the illusion that "it is all over" or as least will be on the 30th December 2020. Five to seven years would be a more realistic prognosis. This based on the longevity of countless other international/global trade agreements. For example; Canada EU, Japan EU, West Africa agreement and indeed the World Trade Organisation.

19/12/19

Reopening of parliament, the Queen's speech largely reflecting the Conservatives manifesto. Boris Johnson and his disciples decidedly gung ho in attitude, whilst Jeremy Corbyn presented himself in much the same way i.e. committed to nothing, adamant about everything. Some blame him for the whole charade, he sat on the fence throughout the EU referendum. Had he followed what was labour policy to remain, before he became leader, the likelihood is, remain would have won the day. 3 years plus on, does anyone have any idea of his leanings leave or remain?

20/12/19

Today is D day, is that D for disaster, is this the beginning of the end, or the end of the beginning? Time will tell. Parliament's last debate and vote of the year. The Bill being a "slightly revised" version of the Withdrawal Agreement Bill (WAB). In general terms these changes relate to employment law, the European Court of Justice and the framing in law of the end date of the transition period. The beginning of the deconstruction of any links with EU law as well as much of the commonality developed between the UK and Europe over 40 plus years of membership. The second nail in the coffin of a free trade deal by next December.

Overnight Andrea Leadsom in her role of Secretary of state for business, energy and industrial strategy, announced the government's approval of a takeover of Cobham, a world leading aero space innovator and manufacturer. This by a United States investment company Advent international, with no apparent synergies to offer. In Boris Johnson's metaphorical cooking terms, is this a nice aperitif for fellow New Yorker Donald Trump? Was this announcement cynically timed to avoid scrutiny, as parliament goes into its Christmas recess? So maybe "D" for deception day is more appropriate?

A Happy New Year

07/01/2020

Parliament reopens, "resistance is futile"

Week commencing 13/01/2020

WBA bill passed though through Commons


Week commencing 20/01/2020

WBA passes House of Lords

WBA passes to the Queen for Royal assent


22/01/20
Trump said that "to embrace the possibilities of tomorrow, we must reject the perennial prophets of doom." This relates to environment and global warming. How does this fit with Michael Gove's environmental agenda?

23/01/22020
USA rejects extradition of Anna Sacoolas who apparently caused the death of a young cyclist in Northamptonshire whilst driving on the wrong side of the road.


24/01/2020
The WAB withdrawal agreement bill is now passed into law completing its journey from the Queen having given the agreement Royal assent.

Next to Downing street to be signed by Boris Johnson Prime Minister and finally Brussels, where it was signed and accepted by Ursula van de Leyen President of the European Council. Perhaps the last nail in the coffin of engagement with the European project. Rather poignant on the anniversary of Winston Churchill's death, the man that dared to suggest;

> "some sort of solution to the European problems could be resolved by creating some sort of United States of Europe" (Zurich 1946)

This now brings Brexit into Sharpe focus, at 11pm on 31$^{st}$ January 2020.

29/01/2020

The EU Parliament today ratified the Withdrawal Agreement, Heir Farage decided to take the opportunity to level a tirade abuse at the European Union in his last speech as an MEP. Suggesting they are bully boys, totally undemocratic and hoped that Brexit would spell the beginning of the end of the EU. He spoke of the rise in Popularist thinking, whilst omitting the word nationalism. Suggesting of course "that Popularism is rising in popularity" Farage at least thought it humorous. This is quite profound coming from the man who is probably the most popular, unpopular man in the land. How many of his Brexit party won seats in the general election? Answer none, attracting only 2% of the electorate's votes. Perhaps the question should be, why does Nigel Farage get such disproportionate exposure from the media?

30/01/2020
The Labour party, seem to be progressing now down to 3/4 candidates, kier Starmer, Lisa Nandy, Rebecca Long-bailey, with Emily Thornberry yet to gain acceptance. Polls are suggesting a shift away from Jeremy Corbyn`s left wing policies, a slightly more centrist move could be advantageous in any future Constituency or General election. Leadership results expected in April

31/01/2020
Well this it, the end of the beginning, the point of no return.

31st January 2020. At 11-00pm The United Kingdom leaves the European Union. Ironically that is midnight central European time. some poignancy there perhaps, whichever side of the debate one takes.

31/01/2020

That is it, we are out of the EU. No bells from Big Ben, just a recording. With poignant pictures of Big Ben and the Houses of Parliament surrounded by scaffold; a symbol of decay, or a symbol of renewal?

Time, it would seem has eroded the cliff edge, leaving just a long and bumpy road to the bottom of the abyss. Is it going to be the promised land, with the new messiah Boris Johnson leading, what could possibly go wrong. Just like Churchill's inspired and motivational speeches, just visualise Boris quoting the 23rd psalm;

> *"Yea, though I walk through the valley of the shadow of death, I will fear no European evil, Dominic Cummings is with me; Jacob Rees-Mogg and Ian Duncan-Smith they comfort me.*
>
> *Donald Trump preparest a table before me in the presence of mine enemies: he anointest my head with a fantastic trade deal; my cup runneth over.*
>
> *Surely schemers and chancers shall follow me all the days of my life: and we will dwell in the house of Trump forever."*

All the promises and commitments have been made, a huge Government majority exists in Parliament. Now is the hour Boris Johnson and company, now you need to deliver. To deliver would unify the nation, even those who thwart you (the remainers), who sincerely hope it's they that have got it wrong. So Boris "get it done" no excuses, no scapegoats, no one to blame. And please don't turn it back on the hard working British people, you have so often patronised.

**Chapter Conclusion**

From the perspective of a pro European project remainer. It would seem that this whole saga is tantamount to snatching defeat from the jaws of victory. Great Britain could have played a very significant part in the development of the European Union creating the Worlds largest trading block second to none. Better a big fish in a big pond, than a small fish in a big pond.

Slightly less than 17 million British people have decided the destiny of the whole of the population, just over 66 million, but this is democracy as we know it. Are we the UK about to embark on The crime of the century?

Words **To Crime of the Century** (Supertramp 1974) **in bold** (Commentary in brackets)

**Now they're planning the crime of the century**
(Boris Johnson is building a master plan for Brexit, immigrants out, Popularist Nationalists in)

**Well what will it be?**
(Britain will be world leaders in free trade, an offshore empire, probably without Scotland and Northern Ireland through the demise of the United Kingdom!!)

**Read all about their schemes and adventuring**
(The daily mail knows best, should be running the country, sees the errors of all, extolling the virtues of Brexit daily)

**Yes, It's well worth the fee**
(Yes it is well worth 60 pence for the football results and the correct date)

**So roll up and see**
(Oh no not a general election again, with the empty promises and hidden agendas)

**How they've raped the universe**
(Donald trump has pulled out of the Paris accord, to make America great again, never mind the pollution)

**How they've gone from bad to worse**
(Telling us the immigrants have taken all the good jobs, ripping off the benefits system and terrorising us)

**Who are these men of lust, greed and glory?**
(Donald trump, Boris Johnson, Dominic Cummings, Jacob Rees-Mogg and the ERG cronies)

**Rip off the mask and let's see.**
(It is not them at all, we see ourselves "the hard working ordinary British people*)

**But that's not right - oh no, what's the story?**
(have we become just like those who we criticise?)

**But there's you and there's me**
(Are we really; self centred, greedy, bigoted, racist, selfish, opinionated, inconsiderate and uncaring beyond our own circles?)

**That can't be right**
(But sadly it is)

# Chapter 5.

## Revelations

Five key factors have emerged from the development of this commentary.

**Age**

**Education**

**Politics**

**Immigration**

**Denial**

## Age

One would have thought that with age, comes a resistance to change. Having been members of the EU for 42 years prior to the referendum, the expectation could reasonably be that, the 60 plus age group would vote to remain in the EU. In this generation's lifetime it is most likely their parents, and quite likely that they themselves were also brought up in Council houses or rented accommodation. The 60 to 80 year old generation were; the pioneers of home ownership, with continuous improvements in standards of living, social mobility, with many travelling the four corners of the planet either with their work or just for a holiday. They have seen their own children with the opportunity to study at universities leading to high pay and professional qualifications. Given that a very significant majority of over 60s wanted to leave the EU, where lies the discontent?

## Education

Stephen kinnock on tvs politics live 16/12/2020 suggested the big divide in the country is between graduates and non-graduates. The big divide being, the graduates who voted remain and the non-graduates voting leave. An interesting thought, that supports findings from researching this narrative, although the question "are you a graduate" was never asked. It was evident in most cases from the jobs people held or retired from. Certainly 90% of business school academics involved in this research were clearly pro-remain. The remaining group of "guesstimated graduates" were circa 70-75% pro-remain.

One could be forgiven for having an expectation that the more educated a person is, then the more likely they are to deliver a well reasoned and accurate conclusion. Within the UK there are circa 14 million graduates and 32 million non-graduates, on the electoral roll. Given Stephen Kinnock`s statement, was the referendum result a foregone conclusion? Clearly many non-graduates voted remain and vice versa. As such it seems worthwhile looking at members of the European Research Group (ERG) who clearly voted for Brexit, and seemingly highly educated. Three key leaders were selected, mainly because of their potential influence on others, particularly their own party members and cabinet members.

**Boris Johnson**      Prime Minister

**Steve Baker**       Chairman of the ERG

**Jacob Rees-Mogg** Leader of the House of Commons

## Boris Johnson

A graduate of Oxford University with a degree in classics. His first job when leaving university was with the Times newspaper as a journalist. According to (Wikipedia 07/02/2020) he was dismissed from this position for falsifying a quotation, seems he has always had difficulty differentiating truth from imagination.

Prior to the referendum and Boris taking the helm of the Brexit campaign. By his own admission wrote two articles for his column in the Daily telegraph, one pro-remain the other pro-leave, he apparently was undecided which to present. So he slept on it overnight, handing in the pro-leave article to the editor in the morning, thus the mould was cast. Clearly a close call for him, but what could have been the deciding factor? Could it have been the rise of popularist nationalism, that provided the enabling mechanism to becoming Prime Minister?

## Steve Baker

Graduated from the University of Southampton with a B'eng in aeronautical engineering. Followed by an Msc in computation from Oxford. He has always been against British membership of the European Union, he tends to hold right wing views. Being anti same sex marriage and would not seem to have too much time for the LGBT lobby. So convinced of his own doctrinaire, he accused civil servants of deliberately producing economic models to direct government policies away from Brexit. When challenged to produce evidence, the absence of which forced an apology. Steve Baker is one of those people in the category of what you see is what you get. His pompous arrogant persona would seem to reflect the person within, pompous and arrogant.

## Jacob Rees-Mogg

A graduate of Oxford Trinity University, with an upper 2nd class degree in history. Rees-Mogg is quite far right in his thinking, some suggest a hard line traditionalist. Apologises for his parties support same sex marriage. Has 6 children, clearly a family man. May 2013, he apparently was invited to speak at the annual dinner of the Traditional Britain Group, a far-right group that suggests non-white Britons are deported. He was advised of the group's leanings, but went ahead suggesting he didn't share their views on this matter. So he certainly isn't frightened of controversy. Net worth well over £100 million (Spears 2019).

So if Steven Kinnock's statement is true i.e. graduates are more likely to be remainers. Why have these clearly highly educated people in such high positions, propagated such a so called hard Brexit?

Boris Johnson opted for Brexit having recognised the rise of popularist nationalism. Coupled to a successful Brexit campaign, conceivably seeing this as a vehicle to the top of the British political tree, Prime Minister. If it all goes wrong, he can always opt out, on the back of his dual nationality to go and live in the wonderland of Trump. What of Boris's reputation, how could he live with failure? Boris is a very shrewd and resourceful man, he doesn't fail, he, always lines up his scapegoats first. "That's what the British people wanted, we live in a democracy, Parliament is there to deliver what the people voted for" etc. Then like a magic trick, the hard working British people turn into lazy, inflexible, resistant to change people that don't know a good opportunity when they see it. That is if it goes wrong of course.

Jacob Rees-Mogg is one of an elitist set, superior in education? breading, intellectually? and wealth. He seeks a status quo akin to that of the "upstairs downstairs" era. where the peasants and working classes knew their place and doffed their caps to their bosses. Rees-mogg does not like the European Union, far too socialist, with their working time directives, national minimum wages, maternity and "God forbid!" paternity pay, safe working practices for employees, dismissal and redundancy protection, pensions and a whole raft other rules designed to undermine business owners. So what does he expect from a hard Brexit, which would seem to be his ultimate aim. Deregulation, opportunities for alternative business activities that don't have tangible products, currency exchange for example. Just consider pre-euro days around 20 plus different currencies in Europe. Look at the buying and selling prices. With a few million pounds buying and selling currency could be a "nice little earner" then of course there are the cross rate variances which provides another avenue to make money. There are many similar mechanisms for virtual products. The more deregulation the more opportunities emerge. One may ask, who are the beneficiaries of these opportunities, well certainly not the hard working British people the government keep telling us about. So Jacob Rees-Mogg is a clever and intelligent man with good reasons to wish for the demise of the European union.

Steve Baker, Oxford yes, Eaton no. Just a well educated hardworking British man with a wannabe mindset. An eagle surrounded by turkeys who doesn't really know the difference.

Clearly there are many well considered reasons for leaving the EU, even from the apparently highly educated, such as the previously mentioned. The potential benefits however for the everyday people of the UK, are very limited it would seem, even with a positive outcome from emerging trade deals.

## Immigration

Of all the topic areas discussed in constructing this narrative, immigration was the most commonly cited reason for leaving the EU. Always at the bottom of the list, but always there, almost as though people were reluctant to bring up the subject until it became the last bastion of their reasoning. Interestingly enough "Lincolnshire voters were among the most Eurosceptic in the UK, with more than 75% of voters in Boston voting to leave" (BBC news) The 2011 census found about 13% of residents in Boston were born in the EU and were largely Eastern-European migrants who arrived after 2004. Is this a coincidence, or perhaps a statement of the real issues? Boris Johnson perhaps recognised this in his referendum campaign of 2016, when;

> *"Johnson repeatedly raised the idea that Turkey – whose application to join the EU had stalled – could eventually become an EU member and its citizens would eventually able to migrate to the UK." (the Guardian 2016)*

Is this contrived scare mongering, that really presses the right buttons for Boris's cause. The 13% plus figure from 2011 likely increased to around 16% by 2016 and this didn't include other immigrants such as Asian or Chinese. This of course put tremendous pressures on the public services, such as schools, hospitals, GP services, police, housing etc. where funding took a minimalistic account of the massive influx of foreign nationals. No wonder the indigenous population took exception to their grossly depleted services and who else can they blame other than the politicians who allowed this to happen? The immigrants of course! This doesn't do much to enable an integrated society. When you see what emigration has done for the indigenous population of the now so called United States of America. The predominantly European immigrants Stole their land, decimated their culture and turned them into second class citizens with rights marginally better than those of animals. Perhaps it isn't too difficult to understand the concerns of those indigenous Lincolnshire inhabitants.

Angela Merkel made a huge error of judgement, as migrants from the Middle East and Africa started to flood into Europe. Many were asylum seekers that were literally fleeing for their lives and desperate for help, protection and shelter. However the majority were economic migrants, acceptably looking for betterment, but completely belligerent to any laws or protocols to deal with those issues. Angela Merkel's error was to let them all in initially followed by vetting and some form of action appropriate to individual needs. From a humanitarian perspective this was on the face of it the right thing to do. This however precipitated new trafficking opportunities for greedy exponents of human misery, turning a wave into a deluge. The migration problem was and is a European problem and needs a European solution. Australian points systems for migration do not apply to asylum seekers, whilst economic migrants won't be too concerned when they are crossing the channel in their boats or stowed away in lorry trailers. When asking interviewees why they considered economic migrants seemed to target the UK. The most common answer given was that the benefits are too easy to get and far too generous. This by implication suggests that benefits within the EU are more rigorous and less generous than those of the UK. So perhaps this is an area where potentially EU rules could have been beneficial to the UK, had they have been adopted. Where immigration goes through a formal process, any points system, is likely to be detrimental to the needs of the UK economy. A very high percentage of work carried out by European migrants is either low skilled or work of a labouring nature, fruit, vegetable, flower pickers, delivery drivers, carwash operators, waiters, chamber maids, cleaners, hotel housekeeping to mention just a few.

Most of these people would not achieve the points required, whilst those that do attain the requirements are not likely to entertain those lesser skilled and lower paid jobs. Some would cite different rules for seasonal workers, but these days most of the seasonal aspects of agriculture and horticulture are diminishing at breakneck speeds, with winter growing crops and the advent of massive all season greenhouses with high efficiency LED lighting. Yes automation is on it's way, but quite limited application at this point in time, and of course very expensive. Ten years down the line virtually total automation is a very likely prospect. The Dutch it would seem are currently at the forefront of this technology.

## Political

The rise of Popularist Nationalism, is a significant factor in the UK'S breakaway from the EU. Unfortunately it would seem the rise in nationalistic thinking is not unique to the UK. Marine Le Pen of the French National Front, Groups like Germany's Alternative für Deutschland (AfD) an anti Muslim organisation, Gabor Vona, the former chairman of the far-right Jobbik and contender for the premiership of Hungary. These and many others with strong ethinic and religious perspectives to their doctrines. The UK of course has its National Front, The English Defence League, UKIP and the SNP although not quite the same ilk as some of the others, but a nationalist party nonetheless. The UK leaving the EU, could potentially provide the catalyst to the demise of both the United Kingdom and the European Union as suggested in previous narrative (pages 85, 160). Even Donald Trump has a nationalist agenda, "make America great again" "America first". This possibility to the detriment of the rest of the world, reopening coalmines, to create more wealth with cheap fuel, more jobs to reduce unemployment. Whilst denouncing as doom-mongers those who seek to protect our planet.

Ignoring the transient political forces, most of the established European Union countries are it is suggested quite centrist, with the Eastern Europe leaning a little right and the west a little left. When the EU has its sensible hat on, it has the potential to step into the driving seat of global leadership, that would of course need to include the UK. Unfortunately it seems the UK will be nailing its flag to the American pole, and with the likelihood of Donald Trump winning a second term. The outcome of which will relegate the UK to become followers and rule takers, not world leaders.

## Denial

According to Merriam-Webster;

> "denial psychology is a "defense mechanism in which confrontation with a personal problem or with reality is avoided by denying the existence of the problem or reality." (7 Nov 2019).

This has been very evident particularly in the proponents and supporters of the Brexit campaign. Where anything that doesn't meet with their expectations is dismissed with comments like "it's just scaremongering" or "more false news". From the many interviews carried out, Brexiteers frequently offered seemingly rational and reasoned responses. These were fundamentally based on conjecture, anecdotal evidence and daily mail reporting, usually framed around, sovereignty, EU rules and immigration. This they believe has been perpetrated by the European Union, with their gravy trains, bureaucracy, and endless rules, Brussels and Strasbourg are dens of iniquity scheming and plotting to rip off the hard working British people.

Well that is what they have been lead to believe by the stalwarts of the "no deal Brexit." More specifically after nearly four years of having Brexit on just about every news item on the radio and television as well as newspapers and magazines people have made up their minds and are totally intransigent to anything that might challenge their stance. If Alan from Viking reads this, I really thought you were going to give me a proverbial "smack in the mouth" when I challenged you relating to the tariffs on lamb issue. Water under the bridge now, and a genuine thank you for your valued input on wider aspects.

## Conclusions

So the key question, why did David Cameron, George Osborne and many supporting academics get the expected outcome of the referendum wrong?

## Age and education

The proportion of graduates amongst over 60s is very significantly lower than their younger counterparts.

The proportion of participating voters is significantly higher in the over 60s group than any other group.

Under 24s were strongly in favour of remain, but the least likely group to actually vote.

The percentage of graduates in the UK has increased from 24% in 2002 to 42% in 2017 this for the 20 to 65 year old group, but of course the majority of graduates are in the younger age groups.

Note: The above ONS (Office of National Statistics) classifications are based on qualifications at HNC (NQF level 4) and above.

## Immigration and politics

Areas of high immigrant influx reflected a disproportionately higher shift to a Brexit vote than any other areas of the country.

This vote it is suggested was more about the immigrants than membership of the EU.

Politicians failed to recognise the concerns of their electors, by failing to invest in infrastructure in terms of schools, to accommodate foreign children with little or English language skills, additional medical provision, housing and community development activities.

Local residents in areas of very high immigrant influx, have very genuine concerns related to the erosion of their local and national culture.

## Politics and denial

Politicians particularly those of the Brexit persuasion have put up so many convoluted arguments, supported by smoke screens and mirrors in abundance.

The benefits gained from membership the EU are quite clear (see STEEPLE Chapter 2)

The benefits of leaving have never been defined in tangible and realistic terms. Apart from a fantastic deal with the USA.

Politicians in a very patronising way, deliberately use highly technical and complex terms to their electors, implying that those not having a full understanding of the context and meaning of their explanation, must be intellectually challenged. Consequently being human, we do not like to be the only person room that doesn't understand, and as a result fail to make a challenge. After around four years of this psychological bombardment many are mentally beaten into submission. In response reverting to kind, digging there heals in and just want to get it done. They become totally averse to engagement with challenge to themselves, as such coming to a state of denial.

Underpinning this psychological onslaught with that of constructed optimism. This perpetrated by first creating an enemy, in this case the European Union. The gravy trains, the bureaucracy, the endless rules, Brussels and Strasbourg are dens of iniquity scheming and plotting to rip off the hard working British people. Then providing the alternative utopia; freedom from EU oppression, making our own rules, fantastic trading opportunities, high wages and so on the list of dreams is endless.

## Summary reasoning

So why did David Cameron, George Osborne and supporting academics such as myself, get the expected outcome of the referendum wrong?

Incorrect assumptions made as follows;

- Older people would not have an appetite for change.
- Levels of education had little or no influence.
- Immigration would only have a moderate impact.
- Time would engender reason, not denial.

## Where are we now.

This concluding section attempts to establish the status quo of Brexit as of 31st January 2020. Due to the dynamic nature of the Brexit process, it is likely that significant events could occur between this date and the date of publication. As far as possible significant events will be included, but only with limited comment.

Earlier in this commentary it was suggested that the UK could potentially lose its 5th position of the GDP hierarchy.

The following list reveals the top ten of World GDPs. For 2019. As predicted earlier in this narrative the UK has slipped from 5th place to 6th place behind India, as opposed to France as expected.

| | | |
|---|---|---|
| United states | 21.439 | Trillion $usd |
| China | 14.140 | Trillion $usd |
| Japan | 5.154 | Trillion $usd |
| Germany | 3.863 | Trillion $usd |
| India | 2.935 | Trillion $usd |
| United Kingdom | 2.743 | Trillion $usd |
| France | 2.707 | Trillion $usd |
| Italy | 1.988 | Trillion $usd |
| Brazil | 1.847 | Trillion $usd |
| Canada | 1.730 | Trillion $usd |
| *Russia* | *1.637* | Trillion $usd |

Source; IMF.org

Projected 2020 IMF (International Monetary Fund) figures suggest France will push the UK down to 7th place. So still maintaining the UKs position in the G7 and G8. Taking the potential loss of Scotland 0.170 T$usd and Northern Ireland 0.053T$usd, could accelerate or even consolidate this event. Russia has been included as a point of interest, but clearly showing those waiting in the wings, although quite a margin at the moment.

HS2 has been given the go ahead, should satisfy some of the ex Labour voters in the north, although a rider has been put on this, with a review next year. Boris has also said China's state railway CCRC has suggested it could build the line in just five years and at a much lower cost. Whilst the Government are suggesting this is world leading technology. It should be remembered the French have had this technology since 1981 with the TGV, on which HS1 is based.

A high court ruling has put a nail in the coffin of the 3rd runway at Heathrow, saying that the environmental criteria used in its evaluation is in direct conflict with the Paris accord on global warming. Unfortunately the same judgment potentially could be applied to the next phases of HS2. Watch this space!

The Labour party leadership election result is expected April 4th 2020. Keir Starmer and Rebecca long-bailey seem to be the front runners at this time, with Jeremy Corbyn doing what he is good at "sitting on the fence."

Boris has thrown his hat into the negotiating ring

with the EU, stating that "if no significant progress is made in negotiations by July" he will be walking away from the negotiating table. The (Guardian 27th February 20) however suggests;

> "If the past is any guide, he will yield in the endgame to the EU but will be too busy taking a victory lap to spell out the concessions he has made."

From the perspective of this ongoing commentary it is still considered that a no deal Brexit result will be the outcome at the end of the transition period December 2020. Boris Johnson and more particularly the ERG, along with Nigel Farage, not only crave the demise of the European Union, but hold Donald Trump's USA in high esteem. As well advocating that a "fantastic" trade deal with the USA is the order of the day.

Considerable effort has been made recently to soften the position on subject areas such as the NHS, chlorinated chicken, hormone fed beef and the like. UK Government sources suggesting that; clear identification of products, would give consumers the choice, "red tractor or star spangled banner"! Or could that be cheap or expensive, which way will the British consumers go?

Donald Trump has said he wouldn't touch the NHS if it were handed to him on a silver platter.

With nearly four years gone since the referendum, one can be forgiven for thinking, there really ought to be more than the two trade deals with the EU and USA on the agenda. Even if only it were with those countries lost as a result of leaving the EU, such as Japan, Canada and the West Africa Agreement countries. Realistically though as a best guess, the USA deal is probably to the stage where just the i's need dotting and the t's need crossing. Trump will win a second term so no problem there. Perhaps a contingency plan could help just in case Donald Trump doesn't win, as unlikely as that is! Although the Corona Virus Pandemic and his handling of the situation could so easily become his Armageddon. So perhaps Boris Johnson and co, ought to start talking to some of those unnamed countries they have spoken of, that are now queuing up to do "fantastic" trade deals with this new dynamic Disunited kingdom.

### The end

The drama continues with the 2$^{nd}$ Edition planned for May/June 2021, this subject to potential changes resultant from the Corona Virus Pandemic.

**Footnote:**

Having read this book for the very last time before publication, and for readers having arrived at this point. I would like to share a moment in time with you. September 2018 standing on the roof of the Reichstag in Berlin, taking in the vast spectacular panoramas, whilst contemplating the frightening events in history that this magnificent building had overseen. Tears rolling down my cheeks my wife of 50 years asked "what ever is wrong", very seldom in my lifetime have I felt so emotional. Being a reflective person by nature, my response was on the following lines;

*"We are standing at the very place, that 73 years ago was conceivably the greatest hub of evil the world has ever known. We now stand here in peace and security, welcomed so warmly by our German friends. The peace, security, freedom and fraternity was won at a very heavy price. Millions gave their lives ridding the world of Nazi tyranny, a triumph of good over evil. This fragile peace needs to be nurtured; this can only be achieved by unity. The rise of Popularist Nationalism, threatens this, the Nuremberg rallies were real, the death camps were real, the millions of dead were real. Why am I so upset? Because I am thinking, have we the human*

*race learned nothing. Are we now so close to arriving at the beginning again?"*

The sincere wish is that "us stalwarts" of the European Project, have "got it wrong," and that Brexit will be a resounding success, allied to the European Union remaining prosperous, peaceful and successful, despite its loss of the UK.

# Appendix

10 questions voters ought to be able to answer.

1. What would happen with the Northern Ireland border with Eire In the event of a no deal Brexit

2. Give three examples of sovereignty representative of the UK.

3. Explain the difference between Duties, Tariffs, Barriers and Quotas with examples.

4. Should the UK continue to contribute to ESA, CERN and Galileo if not what would be the alternatives

5. The UK is not signed to the Schengen agreement what are the implications of this

6. Does the Lisbon treaty 2020 implementation provide more or less democracy for EU members and what is your reasoning

7. Name five or more countries outside the EU that the UK benefits from a trade deal as a

direct result of being a member of the EU

8. What are the trends relating to immigration since the Brexit referendum

9. What are the implications of implementing WTO trade rules to replace those of the European Union

10. Are you able to answer all of these questions with informed and well reasoned responses? If not then do you consider that referendum is appropriate for a critical decision of this gravity.

## Discussion questions

50% of UK trade is with the EU, do we need them?

8% of EU trade is with the UK, do they need the UK?

17 million plus of the UK electorate voted to leave the EU. The population is 66 million plus.

21 million plus of the UK electorate did not vote to leave the EU.

What is the true definition of a majority.

Popularist Nationalism will divide and destroy the human race discuss.

Winning wars when God is on your side is a good thing! Isn't it ?

Now god is on everyone's side, does anyone "win"?

Discuss the following statement;

*"Whilst financial wealth supersedes intellectual wealth, then we are doomed to ultimately fail. The need is to measure success in terms of value to society and not solely monetary metrics. Intellectual value, driven by emotional and ethical values underpinned by some form of measurable dimension is surely the way forward"*! (Anon)

Which 2 major economies present the biggest threat to the status of the USA as the world's biggest economy and why?

## Editors Comments

I have just finished reading this and I think it is brilliant. I read it with an interest for learning, a smile at many of your offhand comments, laughed out loud at the poignancy and humour of your commentary, and had a tear in my eye when I read of the genuine regret and sense of bereavement that you feel over the whole Brexit event in history and its potential impact on the future. Thank you for sharing this with me.

It shows how complex the whole thing is and how ignorant we all are as the electorate (maybe even questions the reliability of democracy-whatever that concept might mean!). Reading it as a diary explained why we all felt a collective sense of despair and confusion; the daily turn of events over the past four years are incredible. Good luck to the future historians! Although with distance, and as part of a bigger story, it may all make more sense.

As you say, I pray we are on the wrong side of history. My biggest fear is that we are not. However, knowing what I know of the younger generation, they are wiser, more resilient, and have a stronger sense of justice and community, alongside a clearer vision for a better world, than we either give them credit for or believe they can achieve. It's a shame we will leave them with many pieces to pick up before they can even start the work of creating a fairer and more sustainable world, but I have every confidence that they will do it...and hopefully they will be the generation which genuinely learns from the past. In the meantime we support them as best we can with their hopes for the future, and we support those who become unwilling victims of the Brexit adventure (directly and indirectly). What else can we do, without the wealth and the power of the elite?

EKH